Regaining VISION

"WHERE THERE IS NO VISION - THE PEOPLE PERISH"

PROVERBS 29:18

BY MICKEY FREED

REGAINING VISION

Available through:
Mickey Freed
Faith Christian Center
1001 Airport Freeway
Bedford, Texas 76021
Phone: (817) 589-8811
Fax: (817) 284-2004
E-mail: faith@faith-center.net

Distributed by:
Faith Christian Center
1001 Airport Freeway
Bedford, Texas 76021

First Printing 2002

ISBN 0-939868-48-2

All scripture unless otherwise noted are from the King James Version of the Bible.

DEDICATION

I would like to give thanks unto the Lord for giving me the strength and the wisdom to comprehend what other people go through so that help could be established in the form of a book. Great appreciation goes to my wife who is an author in her own right, but kept speaking positive things bring me encouragement along the way.

The reason that I have specific feelings of what it is like to have lost vision, is because I have walked through that awful season of my life. I had lost all hope and vision. I can now give God all the glory for allowing me to write something that will bring freedom to someone else. My prayer is that you will read this with great enthusiasm knowing that there is hope even when you feel your vision has died.

CONTENTS

REGAINING YOUR VISION

INTRODUCTION

REGAINING YOUR VISION

The purpose of this book is to help those who have lost vision to get back on track. The loss of vision is a devastating detour that the enemy uses to bring hopelessness and confusion to perhaps an already troubled situation. Without moving forward in God given vision, you will become stagnant in self-fulfillment.

When vision is lost, a person will feel all alone and helpless. Their lifestyles change and they do things that they would not normally do. They turn away from the people that love them the most and usually seclude themselves from all counsel. Not to mention the attacks of the enemy that bring shame, fear, and guilt that pushes them farther into a deep cave.

Proverbs 29:18 says that "people perish without vision". Habakkuk 2:2 says to, "write the vision and make it plain on tablets." It seems that many are guilty of not writing out their personal visions, and thousands are dropping out of the race because they have lost their vision. Many Christians get side tracked by believing a lie of the enemy. The lie goes something like this.

> *They don't need me any more.*
>
> *Many can do what I am doing.*
>
> *Jesus doesn't need me to help.*
>
> *I can never reach my destiny anyway, why try?*
>
> *Life is ok without any friends.*
>
> *My calling was not of God anyway.*
>
> *Nobody cares about me.*

Many who have lost their vision or purpose for living have had these things spoken to them at least once in their lifetime.

The Lord is always moving us from glory to glory; strength to strength. But we must be willing to go through the process of maturing if we are to be transformed.

I have discovered that when someone loses sight of their Godly purpose and vision, they become so disheartened, they have no hope and feel all alone and left out. There aren't many activities that can bring them to repentance except their vision be restored and they return to their "first love".

FOREWORD

REGAINING YOUR VISION

Mickey has presented a vital truth that will bring enlightenment and encouragement to all who want to fulfill their vision from the Lord. He reveals that it is possible to have vision and yet lose it. Some never become knowledgeable of their commission from God. A vision is the revelation from God stating that we have been called to accomplish a certain thing in our lifetime. It is a divinely directed goal with an objective to be reached. A God given vision gives us hope and a future. Vision gives enthusiasm and steadfastness to life. As long as an individual has vision they have motivation and direction for life.

However, mankind can go through certain experiences that can cause their vision to fade. Discouraging things can happen until the vision is obscured and lost forever. While reading Mickey's transcript, I realized that our vision is like the sail on a sailing ship. It is not the ocean waves or the blowing of the wind that determines the direction of the ship but the set of the sails. Like the sails, it is the setting of our vision that determines the way our life goes. Sails can be set where they can catch the wind and propel the ship toward the captains desired destination.

Like the captain of a ship, we can set the sails of our mind and our hearts. The waves of circumstances and winds of discouragement will not determine our attitude and destiny, but the set of our vision. If the captain loses his sails and has no oarsmen, then he is left afloat on the ocean of life with no way to direct his ship. If a person loses his vision he has no way to properly direct his sails if he is ever to reach his destination.

Mickey shows us how to know our vision and how to reactivate vision if it is lost. The truths shared within this book can make a difference in a person's destiny. God bless you Mickey for sharing these vital truths with us from your revelation of the Word and life experiences.

Dr. Bill Hamon

PREFACE

REGAINING YOUR VISION

A few years ago I seemed to be under an attack of the enemy but did not realize as a believer in Jesus Christ I could lose my vision and purpose for God. I am and was a strong believer in the Word and ministered with the revelation of Christ. Yet one day while on vacation, I awoke and found myself designing golf courses. I had no enthusiasm to serve God any longer. My body was tired, my attitude was tired, my thoughts were tired and I was tired of everything. I had <u>no vision</u> to fuel me any longer. I did not want anyone talking me out of my decision. And to top everything else, there were other little problems and I did not want to deal with them. I called my oversight and told them that if they had someone to take over my responsibilities it would be fine with me. I was throwing in the towel; my fight was over.

My <u>vision</u> was gone. No hope. No trust. No theological studies could bring me to where I needed to be. It wasn't my duties or job. It wasn't anyone or anything in particular. It was the enemy trying to discourage me to draw me away from my calling and destiny. What I needed was a Word from the Spirit of the Lord.

It was then that the Lord spoke and said, "Go back and prepare. Rewrite your vision and keep your eyes on me for surely I shall do a new thing".

I am so thankful that I did not totally quit. The enemy has tried many different tactics but "Regaining Vision" and getting back on track was my hardest quest. I am proud to report that we are doing better than ever and God is still ruling and reigning in our lives.

Vision is the very heartbeat of everyone who is trying to succeed in his or her destiny. Vision is the force that thrusts you beyond the darts of the enemy day by day. Vision is the fuel and energy that motivates us to accomplish our everyday tasks. Without vision people really do perish!

CHAPTER ONE

HOW CAN I GO ON?

Day after day we meet challenges head on and sometimes the challenges seem to be more than we can handle. We stumble around hoping and praying that our God will intervene and pull us out of this pit that we seem to have fallen into. Or at least it seems as if we have lost our hope and our destiny. Life has its struggles and almost always has a way of bringing us to a place of repentance.

We find ourselves like Job crying out to God but it seemed as if God was nowhere to be found. Although Job stood his ground and all the while he was going through his testing, we find that Job never lost his vision of God. God was making sure the enemy was constantly giving Him reports and information daily. The enemy can only talk a good talk, but it is God who was ultimately in control all the time.

It seems that our struggles with trials and tribulations are coming from the very pits of hell, but yet in our spiritual maturity, we are supposed to know how to handle these trials so that we don't become pulled away from our vision.

The enemy is always looking for that weakness in our lives so that he can challenge our *"faith."* It is our faith that has to come to the top when we are walking through a storm. Our faith is the substance that supports our destiny and vision. Without faith it is impossible to please God. (Heb. 11:6)

In Second Timothy, Paul says to Timothy:

Verse 7: "We are ever learning, and never able to come to the knowledge of truth."

Apostle Paul said that we would have perilous times and that we would not be able to avoid them. We must remember it is the times of testing that push us to another level.

In every level of Christianity there seems to be a storming process. That process occurs when we are in the times of testing. God brings forth maturity by allowing circumstances to test our ability and character. It seems that when our circumstances become dry and unstable, that's the time when our spiritual growth is increased.

> *It is our faith that has to come to the top when we are walking through a storm.*

Did you ever stop and think how God uses the enemy to do His work to get us where we need to be? Sometimes we are hard of hearing, stubborn, and want to hold on to those blind spots so that we will not be responsible for our actions. Aren't you glad that our God is a God of grace and understanding? There are times in our lives when it seems that as soon as we get over one *process*, we begin a new one. And sometimes we don't know if it is God working on us or it is the enemy working on us. How do we know the difference?

In the book of Luke chapter 22, we see how the disciples began a journey one *"certain day"*. I don't know about you but I have had those certain days when it seems like the forces of hell were trying to plow me under. I know who I am in Christ, yet it seems that he *(the enemy)* is no respecter of Christians. The more I cry out for the anointing of God, the more it seems I am attacked. The enemy is always attacking anyone with an anointing because it is the anointing that destroys the yokes and bondages. (Isaiah 10:27). I feel that not only was Jesus' disciples anointed, but they had the anointed one with them in the boat.

Jesus had told them:

Luke 8:22 "let's go over to the other side."

When Jesus says that you are going over to the other side, there may be all kinds of storms that come against us, but if Christ told us, then we have the assurance that we will reach our destiny on the other side. Without fail, there can be nothing that can stop you when Jesus is with you. There may be high winds, high waves, hard rain, even a hurricane, in the spiritual sense, but there will be nothing to stop you from reaching your destiny.

NATURAL VS. SPIRITUAL STORMS

During storms your sense of direction can be easily lost. When your direction is lost because of a storming process such as discontentment, oppression, hopelessness, or other trials; you must go back to your vision. It is your vision that is the very tool that keeps you on track. For instance, a sailor must use proper instruments when navigating the seas to prevent danger or to stay on course. An airplane pilot should be licensed with a rating of *"instrument flight rating"* (IFR) to keep his plane on course when flying at night or perhaps during stormy weather. When a pilot flies by their natural eyesight, it is called *"visual flight"*. They can fly anywhere that they can see. But if they find themselves in a storm or possibly cloudy weather, they can become disoriented quickly and lose their sense of direction. Many pilots crash because they become confused and lose their sense of direction because they cannot visually see where they are going.

Some people fly spiritually everyday by only what they see in the natural. When a storm comes, they begin to be blown off course and find themselves spiraling toward the earth. The storm has prohibited them from seeing what is real and where they are going. They have feelings but their feelings are not real.

Their vision has been clouded and therefore what they can't see is no longer of value. The very thing that was keeping them on course is now nowhere to be seen. They have no intuition or stability to keep them air borne.

Your vision is your instrument rating for pulling you out of storms. When you are unable to see because your mind has become distracted, get back to your vision. Stay focused. Hold on to your hearts desire. Remember where your heart is, that is where your treasure will be. Your vision has not been forsaken; you are only going through a storm.

If we as children of God expect only to soar with the Lord only when our vision is clear, then we are only setting ourselves up for failure. We are the ones that must stay focused. We are the ones that must prepare ourselves to go through the storms. We would be foolish to think that we would never need "IFR" rating in the spiritual sense when the enemy is forever trying to keep us in storms. If the enemy can keep our eyes blinded spiritually from our vision, then we will perish in despair.

Our spiritual instruments that we use during storms are prayer, discernment, word of wisdom, word of knowledge, and other spiritual tools that keep us from sinking and/or keep us soaring with Christ.

Storms in the natural can come from any direction. They range from a windy-blowing rainstorm, to us having to take shelter because of its velocity or force.

When spiritual storms come, they seem to come suddenly out of nowhere just as quickly and have somewhat the same effect as the natural storms. We don't know whether to fight or take shelter. Our vision is under attack, which leaves us with only our instruments to battle the ranging spiritual storm.

Spiritual storms seem to have no mercy on us because we are believers. But one thing we do know is this; God is somewhere in the middle of this storm and I must find the center of His will. And at the center of His will, we find our vision.

Let us compare the natural storms with spiritual storms so that we can see more clearly. For example, during some of our Texas storms the wind is boisterous and the dust is swirling. Immediately following the boisterous wind, the rain begins to fall slowly, but steadily becomes heavier and heavier. There are times when it is necessary to pull over and stop when driving because of no vision in the natural.

Even in the midst of a spiritual storm our minds can become cloudy. There can be so much noise a person can't hear the voice of the Lord. Even though a spiritual noise may not be loud, there seems to be an assignment against our minds that does not allow us to think properly. Therefore, I think it is wise when a person does not have clear direction, especially during a stormy season of their life, to call upon a multitude of counsel. Spiritually when the voice of the Lord is not clear, or when there is no peace, we should slow down and look for road signs along our pathway. It is the signs of the Lord that prevent us from winding up in a ditch in the middle of nowhere. Sometimes in the spiritual we need to park our spiritual motors and STAND until the storm passes.

> *If the enemy can keep our eyes blinded spiritually from our vision, then we will perish in despair.*

One of the enemy's greatest tricks is to put spiritual blinders on you so that your vision will be lost. Your vision cannot be seen because you cannot even see tomorrow, much less plan your future. You cannot think of anything other than where you are at the present time.

There have been great spiritual sailors that have lost their way in the midst of thriving storms. Without the proper equipment, it would be impossible for them to return to their original position. We must remember spiritually,

"Smooth seas never make a good sailor".

When battling storms whether they are spiritual are natural, we must ask ourselves two things. Number one, "How did I get here?" And number two, "How do I get myself out of this?" In either battle we must depend on the Lord to pull us out.

If storms keep occurring over and over, it could be that the Lord is strengthening you or perhaps trying to bring change. Let me explain.

If you are in a winter season and it seems to be dry don't become unreachable because you are not seeing any fruit. Trees may lose their leaves in the wintertime but their roots grow deeper and deeper. Why? Because come next spring the tree is required to produce more fruit. The roots must be deeper to pull more nourishment for it will be required to produce more fruit the following year. The bigger the tree, the more resistance it must have against turbulent winds and storms. The more mature you become in the Lord, the more fruit is expected. Whom much is given, much is required. The bigger your vision, the bigger the storms of adversity will come against you. Your roots must continue to grow deeper and deeper.

Remember not much fruit is grown in dry soil. Therefore, there must come a change in order for your vision to begin to grow and mature. The change doesn't have to be a location change or a natural move; it could be as simple as re-submitting yourself again spiritually to your family church. Usually in dry seasons only a couple of things biblically are probable. First, the Lord is trying to push our roots deeper so that we can be more fruitful. Or secondly, He is trying to get us to move so that our vision does not die. Although distinguishing between these two can be confusing at times, if we follow vision, they can be easily distinguished. It is because we lose vision of where we are headed that makes these choices difficult.

THE JEZEBEL SPIRIT

One of the most vicious spirits that cause visions to be lost is the Jezebel Spirit. For example, let us take a look at Elijah who ran into the wilderness after hearing the report of Jezebel.

It was a day's journey in the wrong direction until he rested under a juniper tree; totally exhausted and cried out to the Lord to die. As he lay under the juniper tree praying to die, an angel came and brought him a warm freshly baked cake with a cruise of water and said, "arise and eat". It wasn't until the angel had touched him the second time that Elijah ate the freshly baked cake. Elijah still didn't get the full vision for he went forty days and forty nights on a freshly baked cake and a cruise of water but still wound up in a cave that was in Mt. Horeb. When the Lord asked him, "What doest thou here, Elijah?" Elijah answered and said that, "He alone was left and the people of Israel had forsaken the covenant and the prophets have all been slain by the sword of Jezebel." But the Lord spoke not by the wind, earthquake, or fire, but in a small still voice and instructed Elijah to *return* the way that he came. Upon returning, he was to anoint Hazael as king over Syria. And while there, anoint Jehu to be king over Israel and anoint Elisha as his successor.

What a prime example of someone who lost their vision because the enemy had blinded their natural wisdom and had separated them from understanding the purposes of God. The Lord knew Elijah's strengths and weaknesses and yet used him in the midst of his weakness and strengthened him to *return* to his present vision and allowed him to finish his task. Hazael was to be anointed king of Syria. Jehu was to be anointed king over Israel. And the mantle of the prophet was to be passed on to a successor so that double portion miracles could take place. What a disaster it would have been for Elijah if he had been disobedient to the vision of the Lord. It was the Jezebel spirit that drove him to the wrong place and put the spirit of discontentment in his heart.

> *Just because someone has a character flaw of being pushy or persistent does not necessarily place him or her into a category of Jezebel.*

I believe it would help if you knew some of the tactics of this spirit. Elijah was facing a major problem that he had not faced before. We see people today losing vision and running from the very thing God has ordained them to do. But because of the spirit of Jezebel, they lay it all down and turn to something a bit less complicated.

Most people relate the Jezebel spirit as being a lady wearing lots of makeup and along with the war paint comes a pushy, driven person. Please remember that just because someone has a character flaw of being pushy or persistent does not necessarily place him or her into a category of Jezebel. However, it is one of the character flaws of a person under the influence of a Jezebel stronghold.

THE JEZEBEL SPIRIT

Ten Things the Jezebel Spirits do:

1. Stifles or suffocates God's Spirit.
   (Tries to stop the spirit of the Lord)

2. Undermines God's Leaders.
   (Starts gossip and other stories about others)

3. Falsely accuses God's Leadership
   (Brings false accusations & lies against leaders)

4. Manipulates itself into key positions
   (Especially praise and worship)

5. Brings confusion into intercessory prayer
   (Manipulates themselves into position)

6. Binds up and strangles finances
   (Spiritual bondage & confusion during breakthroughs)

7. Wants to be seen and heard
   (Starts a rumor so it can stir up strife among leaders)

8. Tries to create spiritual ceremonies
   (Not God inspired)

9. Opens doors for strife and disloyalty
   (Causes confusion among the sheep)

10. Speaks against God's Word
    (Tries to gain control of a matter by having a better way)

Elijah was running but running from what? The Jezebel is a harassing controlling spirit that will separate you from destiny and vision. Its control and manipulation suffocates you and steals everything that gives you life. The three major signs for recognizing a Jezebel spirit is control, manipulation, and seduction. Usually where there is a Jezebel, there is an Ahab. An Ahab is a person that allows that spirit to accomplish its mission but puts up no resistance. The Jezebel spirit will go to any means to accomplish its goals. It will use legalism, deception, self-perfection, self-pity, and even witchcraft to overcome its obstacles.

Even though Elijah had a prophetic word from the Lord, the Jezebel spirit was able to convince him to forget about his mission. Even after all the miracles the Lord performed through him, this spirit was able to confuse him and even cause suicidal thoughts.

We too allow fear to come upon us during our times of challenges. But we cannot allow a Jezebel spirit to challenge us with fear and be manipulated and controlled to the point that we lose our vision and purpose for living.

If the enemy can convince you to become a loner and never submit to accountability, your vision could possibly never succeed in the eyes of God. It was the *return* of Elijah's heart that put him back on vision again. We must remember that God has purposely placed a vision of the gospel in every heart so that His vision can successfully be implemented through us. If the enemy can separate God's vision from our vision there could be people who will never come to know the Lord Jesus Christ. That is a staggering thought, but I wonder how many people will miss the rapture simply because Christians lost their vision and fell away from the calling of the Lord in their lives. Impartations were never imparted, their anointing was never used, their talents never reproduced. Their ministry withered away because of loss of vision.

Before we conclude this thought, there is one note that might be of value to you. The Lord still provided for Elijah even though he ran in the wrong direction. The Lord will never leave us or forsake us. It is we who always leave the anointing and get forsaken because of our disobedience or circumstance. Even though Elijah had strayed away from his main vision, the Lord never left his side. As we all have strayed from God's purpose in our lives, it is comforting to know that the Lord is a God of a second chance.

UNATTAINABLE VISION

There are people and churches today that have been trying to achieve a vision for years but have only been able to accomplish a small portion of fulfillment. This is not to say that they haven't tried to accomplish destiny. But without the proper people, money, and leadership abilities, it becomes more difficult to establish and complete a vision.

Sometimes a vision that is unreachable is a vision that is too far fetched. It is better to have a vision that can be achieved over months or years and then extend the vision, than to have a vision that is unattainable.

When vision is delayed we must be careful not to forget our destiny. Sometimes a delayed vision that has been placed before us can become old manna. And we all know what happens to old manna. It becomes rotten and unfit for the next day. We should never take lightly the vision that the Lord has placed upon our hearts to achieve.

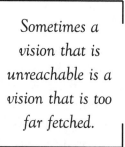

Sometimes a vision that is unreachable is a vision that is too far fetched.

When an opposition comes to detain us, the first thing that we must ask ourselves is, *"Where are we spiritually?"* Usually our first thought is to get out! The second thought is "How can I go on"? Our hope has been deferred because we have lost vision. To make a change spiritually verses making a natural change to satisfy the flesh, is never the right choice. Since our flesh does not like to be uncomfortable, we make a spiritual change. God is trying to bring us to a place of destiny in Him, so the enemy attacks our vision.

If vision is lost, then you may be in need of your oversight to speak vision back into your life. It is very important to get proper counsel when loss of vision occurs. Getting proper counsel means that you go to your pastor or counselor and not the lady or gentleman next door. They may have good insight but you are in need of spiritual counsel that has like vision. For example, if you have one belief in God and someone else has different beliefs in the Lord, then you will get mixed counsel on how to get your life back. When loss of vision is occurring or has occurred, this is not a time to get mixed counsel from everyone that you meet.

Proverbs 29:18

"Where there is <u>no vision</u>, the people perish:"

Praise the Lord for proper oversight! I thank the Lord for men and women of God that are *true* spiritual leaders that will give proper oversight and bring us into accountability so that our vision will not be lost. If we are in the middle of the storm we might be thinking that the storm is all over and we are just sitting in the eye of the storm. Yes it is calm, but the back of the storm is yet to pass. That is why sometimes it feels like we just came out of one storm and now we are in another. It is not another storm, just the first one completing its path. Hopefully with proper equipment like faith, love, encouragement, hope, and strength; you will move back onto your road again to achieve your vision. Remember that during storms things get uprooted. The Lord uses storms to clear out the unnecessary items that can cause us failures down the road.

I believe that the Lord allows certain storms or challenges to push us to another level. Without challenges or resistance we don't build bigger muscles. The more times we flex our muscles with a heavier object than just our arm, the stronger or more toned our muscles become.

Without having to pray and wage war against the wicked one, we become ingrown to our environment and there is no transformation that leads us toward our destiny. We have become as the caterpillar that never found his way to a good tree - that never found the right leaf - that never was high enough off the ground - that was never strong enough. Besides all of these obstacles, the tree was too far away in the first place.

As believers, we must guard our minds from being deceived by the enemy that enables us to blame everyone and everything around us except ourselves. Apostle Paul said in Romans 12: 2 that we are not to be conformers but transformers.

Romans 12:2

"And be not conformed to this world: but be ye transformed by the renewing of your mind, that ye may prove what is that good, and acceptable, and perfect, will of God."

Our vision is so important that without it we lose our way. When storms come, we must know that Jesus is in the boat. When brooks dry up, we know that it is time to move on. When we move on, our vision is getting closer to being fulfilled. After all, it is not how many storms we endure. It is how many storms will it take to get us to the right place so that the blessings of our Father can be poured out on us.

We often ask ourselves, *"How can I go on?"* However, our confession needs to be, "I have destiny inside of me. Transform me as I walk through my experiences so my vision can be reached."

How can we go on? We can go on because God has placed a determination within us called "Vision". Vision is what keeps us on target. Vision is the substance that has not been accomplished or obtained, but is the element that propels us into destiny.

► **Prayer to help regain vision:**

Father I am willing to go through any process that will put me back in touch with your purpose and plan. My vision is lost. My hope is deferred. Therefore I am confessing that I have lost my vision. Help me Lord. I am not strong enough by myself to regain your vision that you placed in my heart. I need your help to connect myself back into the race. I do not want to miss the mark. I have allowed self-pity to come upon me and seclude me from the work of the Lord. Even though I feel alone, I know that you are always with me. You would never leave me or forsake me. My fellow friends at my ministry love me and I have deserted them. Lord I pray your word over myself right now. I am a child of the King. I have all power over the enemy. (Luke 10:19) Lord I am picking back up where I left off and I will not allow the forces of darkness to convince my mind to stray again. I have the mind of Christ. My words that go forth out of my mouth will not return unto me void but will accomplish that which I say, and the words will prosper in the very thing where I send them. (Isaiah 54:11) Devil, you are a liar and a deceiver. I have found you out. Therefore, get the behind me, for I have a vision to fulfill. AMEN!!!

CHAPTER TWO

LOSS OF VISION

I was on my way home from the grocery store when I realized that I was heading in the wrong direction. We had just sold our home and we were living in a different city.

Our *"new home"* wasn't but a few miles from our old one but in different metropolitan area. In a large city it is common to have several smaller municipalities that are land locked within a larger city. Therefore, you can travel from one municipality into another and never know that you have left your present city. My soulish nature was leading me to the *"old place"* but I didn't live there any more.

Some of you have been in the same situations before and may have never realized it. You were headed to the local pizza place, but you ended up in a food store instead. You didn't realize you were going an *"old way"* until you got there.

If we allow our minds to focus on an old feeling or an old thought it can easily lead us down the path heading in the wrong direction. I have found that when I end up in an *"old place"* it is because I have let my mind focus on the past.

When we allow our minds to wonder aimlessly without taking our thoughts captive (II Cor. 10:5), we could wind up in a real spiritual mess.

II Cor. 10:5

"Casting down imaginations, and every high thing that exalteth itself against the knowledge of God, and bringing into every captivity every thought to the obedience of Christ."

According to the word, every thought has to be taken captive. Too many ungodly thoughts clutter our minds. Too many subjects fill our minds. Our minds will most often focus on our past failures rather than our future potential. Why is that? I personally think it is because life experiences mark our minds for the worse. There are many scars of our past. If we have had a bad experience that brought pain, then we are more likely to remember such an experience because of the dramatic effect that it made on our lives. Good experiences are remembered as well, but it seems as if the bad experiences out weigh the good.

Why is this important to know? Because when you have loss of vision, *"old"* things begin to re-occur in our thoughts. Our memory recalls the hurt, the loss, and/or the dramatic recollection of the painful events. Loss of vision occurs because we allow the remembrance of *"old things"* to overtake our thought process and as a result our immediate values become more important to us than our vision. Like a computer, our minds have the ability to recall an old memory like it was yesterday. Our minds are as the mind of Christ but somehow we allow a negative thought or an old thing to filter into our thought process and we begin to move backward instead of pushing the delete button and erasing the pain from our memory chip. Our mind does have the ability to forget, but because of spiritual hurts and loneliness, we seem to hold on to an *"old thing"* even though we have repented for our shortcomings. I believe we can choose to stay where we are, *(a dead place)* or we

> *Our minds will most often focus on our past failures rather than our future potential.*

can choose life. We can remain as a victim or we can choose to accept the victory. I have found that the Lord will allow me to stay wounded and hurt as long as I choose to remain there. Self-pity is just another stronghold of the enemy.

WITHOUT VISION WE PERISH

When loss of vision comes we must remind ourselves that without vision we perish. Vision releases us into transformation and transformation releases life. We perish because we have lost hope of our destiny.

Have you ever stumbled in the dark not being able to see? When we are not able to see with our natural eyes, we begin to be unsure of our next step. In the natural darkness without light we stumble around because we can't see. There is lack of natural vision.

In the spiritual, we do the same things but sometimes we are not aware of our own stumbling. Some call it confusion. Others call it being overwhelmed. Regardless of what a person may call it, there is a loss of sight of where you are going.

One of the greatest challenges of your life will be to hold on to your vision. The enemy comes to steal, kill, and/or to destroy. He will attack and focus on every weakness and opportunity we open to him. We must pray that the Lord will give us wisdom and discernment to know our weaknesses and strengths.

I have found that by taking one step at a time helps me stay on track.

In the Old Testament, history tells us that many of the saints would tie lanterns around their ankles as they walked at night so that they could see the next step. They were not considering the miles ahead of them, but only their next step. They could not concentrate on what was even a few yards ahead of them because they were only considering the next step.

As you journey thru life, we must not be concerned so much

about next year or even next week. But we must keep ourselves on track by taking one step at a time. When we lose vision we should not worry about our long-range goals but rather focus our thoughts on one day at a time. After we begin to gain momentum, then and only then, are we once again able to see our vision back into full focus.

Do not allow the enemy to sow lies into your mind such as, you have failed; you won't make it; you're not strong enough; you're too weak; they won't miss you if you leave; and so on. We should realize by now when our vision is cloudy and spiritual tiredness weighs upon us, we are not to make any quick decisions. Quick decisions are usually made out of our soulish realm. Making quality decisions while your vision is being threatened is not wisdom. Most of the time when quick decisions are made without prayer and the peace of our Lord, they are wrong.

In the book of Habakkuk he wrote;

Habakkuk 2:2

"Then the LORD answered me and said: 'Write the vision and make it plain on tablets, That he may run who reads it.'"

Notice that it said, *"write the vision"*. Writing your destiny is very important and it enforces the fact that you have a goal and a destiny. It is vision that enlightens your path so that you will not stumble around for years and get nothing accomplished.

WRITE THE VISION

When writing our vision we begin to see where we are going. Some people may call it goal setting but our vision is more than writing something that we intend to accomplish. Your vision is what the Lord has placed in your heart. Everyone is different and your vision will be strictly for you. Notice that your personality is different than the next person. You think differently. You talk differently. We are all made differently but made in the image of our God. The Lord has never intended for you to be like anyone else, therefore your vision is personal.

Parents sometimes tell their children, *"Why can't you be like your sister or brother"?* We can't be like our sister or brother because they are made differently. Although we know what the parent is trying to say, they express a verbal expression to get you to act as nicely as perhaps your brother or sister.

God has placed and developed within every person a substance of goodness. When we sin, the opposite of goodness begins to appear. Unless we repent and turn from our wicked ways, the Lord will not heal our land. (II Chronicles 7:14). Meaning, that we have opened a door for the not so good things to infiltrate the goodness that the Lord has placed within us. When our vision begins to become less than our achievements, then we are driven and not led. Your vision is not big enough. Let me give you an example.

> *We can remain as a victim or we can choose to accept the victory.*

Let us say that an architect's vision was to build an office building that was forty stories high. He drew the plans and was able to raise the millions of dollars to accomplish his vision. Two years later he would drive by and see his vision standing forty stories high.

There remains a question that we must ask ourselves. Was this one building his vision or was his vision to build forty-story office buildings? The difference is this. If the one building was his vision, then his vision has been completed or fulfilled. But if he has a vision to draw and erect office buildings, his vision has only begun. We should never allow ourselves to be driven past our vision. If you accomplish your vision too quickly, then you must enlarge your vision.

It is vision that enables you to push through circumstances that would normally pull you down. It is your written vision that takes you to your next level.

If you lose your vision, you lose sight of your next step. Not only do you lose your sight but also you lose hope. The word says, "Hope deferred makes the heart sick."

Proverbs 13:12

"Hope deferred makes the heart sick, but when the desire comes, it is a tree of life."

When a person loses hope, the heart becomes an issue. Jesus often spoke of the heart being the center point of knowledge. Just as He spoke of the "rivers of water coming from the belly or the inner part of our being," so it is when we speak of the heart. Apostle Paul tells us in the book of Romans in chapter ten that we are to confess with our mouths and believe in our hearts that Christ has arisen from the dead. (Romans 10:9-10) If we only have head knowledge then we can easily be deceived. But if we believe with our heart *(a knowing)* then we can hold on to the truth and the truth can bring back our "first love" which includes our destiny in God.

Our loss of vision can make us feel as though we have dropped off the edge of disaster. Without vision we seem to wander around hopelessly with our heads down and feeling sorry for ourselves. The more someone asks how you are doing, the more we plunge into our pits and wonder how we got there. As we are falling hopelessly into our self-pity, feeling lost and unsecured, fear seems to find its way into our vacant lives. After all, we have allowed the enemy to distract us by using someone or something to pull us away from what gives us life; our vision. And now we find ourselves with no hope, no destiny, no goals, and certainly NO VISION. Where are we to land? Where have we plunged from and where are we fleeing too?

> *We should never allow ourselves to be driven past our vision.*

A JOURNEY OF FLESH

When vision is lost we often take a pathway that feels as if we are in total control. But this journey is only a short journey of the flesh. The flesh will always carry you where you feel the most comfortable. This comfort zone should alarm us like a flag waving in the wind. You are not headed in the right direction but headed down a road of destruction. We think it is safe, comfortable, pleasing, and even fulfilling, but this journey will not last long because it is the very opposite of the spiritual. The natural or (self) has over ridden the spiritual. If vision and hope are not regained, your valley journey will only become deeper and deeper. Even though everything seems to be pleasing to self, you're wondering further from your vision and purpose.

Take Jonah for instance. God was trying to use him to deliver a word to the city of Nineveh, and he begins his expedition by trying to run from the presence of the Lord. Jonah runs to Joppa and found a ship going in the opposite direction. Little did the sailors know that they were allowing a fugitive to board their ship. When a storm came and the boat began to be filled with water the sailors began frantically to throw equipment and food overboard to lighten their load. They then sought to find Jonah only to find him sleeping in the middle of a storm. Jonah tells them to take him and throw him overboard and the storm will cease. He confessed running from the God that made the wind and the sea. They ignored Jonah and tried to row harder and harder but was unsuccessful in their endeavor.

We are not so different. When our vision is lost, we begin running from God. Some may say, "I would never run from the Lord!" But when you are running from the vision that the Lord placed in you, YOU are running from God. If the Lord needed someone else to fulfill the vision in your heart, He would have chosen someone else instead of you. He doesn't make mistakes. He is God. He loves change, but never changes.

(Mal. 3:6) But because of circumstances, what ever that may be, we seem to want to quit on the Lord. I am so glad that He never quits on us, aren't you?

The sailors finally consented and threw Jonah overboard and the storm ceased. As the story goes, a great fish swam by *(that the Lord had prepared for Jonah)* and swallowed Jonah up. For three days Jonah was on a fast. Some may say, what fast? Well, I don't know about you but I would not want to eat what a fish ate last night. Especially seaweed!

Anyway, Jonah is in the hands of the Lord. In the belly of a great fish Jonah begins to repent and the Word says that the Lord heard him. As the fish vomits him out upon dry land, the Lord picks up exactly where He left off and told Jonah to "arise and go to Nineveh."

I think that this is a great lesson here for those who have lost their vision. Firstly, the lord may allow you to wander for a season, but there will come a time when the Lord will cause a storm to come to put you back on the right track. Secondly, I believe that if we should stray from the purpose of the Lord, He always seems to start us where He wants us to start. We sometimes argue with God and try to convince Him that we have already been this way before, but He seems to always know what we need and where we need to start. Jonah could run but he could not hide. After obedience and submission, Jonah found himself at the place of beginnings once again.

We should not fear submission to God. Anytime fear is allowed to penetrate our faith we find ourselves searching for the real truth. The point being, you already have and know the truth, but the enemy blinds us with fear, and you feel as if you have lost your way. When the spirit of *fear* comes, it is usually coupled with *doubt* and *unbelief* as well. This "trio" spirit can reap spiritual havoc when teaming together. It is no secret in spiritual warfare that these three travel together. Fear is the opposite of faith and fear causes us to feel defeated and useless. Sometimes fear manifests itself under the disguise of confusion. This is when we need to pray. Prayer will disarm a spirit of fear and you'll find your vision returning.

THE SNARE OF THE ENEMY

Man is a three part being, body, soul, and spirit. Satan always aims his attack at the two weakest parts of man. The soul and the flesh. He attacks the soul because this is where choices have to be made. He attacks the flesh because this is the part of man that does the physical bidding. And since the body contains the presence of Christ, the enemy looks for weaknesses in our flesh so that he can tear down the vision and destiny that God has placed within us. If he can weaken your body, then he is weakening the plan of God through you.

The enemy is always attacking the very nature of God through man. By challenging and testing man satan finds our weaknesses and strengths.

One of the ways that the enemy weakens man is through confusion of words. Satan often brings confusion to men and women with words that they are familiar with, but the meaning of the word may be totally different than they think. The words that we hear may sound Godly but the enemy recognizes that one of our weaknesses is not defining what we hear. Most of the time when we hear a spiritual sound we immediately assume that it is of the Lord. Let us look at the scripture to bring clarity to this point.

> *If you lose your vision, you lose sight of your next step.*

In chapter four of the book of Luke, we read where Jesus being full of the Holy Ghost, is being led into the wilderness by the Spirit of the Lord. The word *"led"* is *"a-go"* in the Greek; meaning to be lead away or to accompany while being lead away. In verse nine we read that the enemy *brought* Jesus to a high place in the temple. The key in this passage is the word *"brought"* which means in Greek to be lead away or to accompany while being lead away. That's right you guessed it. Although the words are different, they are being used by two separate sources but have the same meaning. The Holy Ghost is using one and the enemy is using the other. Many times the enemy brings a counterfeit word to us and we don't check our spiritual discernment, therefore are led astray and are *brought* to a spiritual place by the wrong spirit. I had rather be led by the Holy Spirit than be brought to a certain place by the enemy. The enemy would like for you to think that his power by accompaniment, means the same as the Holy Spirit. The enemy has always been a deceiver and always will be.

> *When you are running from the vision that the Lord placed in you, YOU are running from God.*

We have been taught that the enemy is a liar and a copycat. This fact only confirms that the enemy cannot do anything in the original form. Of course it did not work with Jesus because He saw that it was a counterfeit. If the enemy will try to use his counterfeit lies on Christ, he will try to use them on Jew and Gentile alike. He is no respecter of persons.

When someone has lost their vision and hopelessness has set in, it is easy for them to be deceived. How easy it is for satan to bring deception to us when using words that sound like God. If it sounds like God and it feels like God then most of the time we consider it to be God.

The truth is we love our God and would never be disobedient to our calling or vision. But when vision is lost, we should lean not to our own understanding. If we were on track with the Lord, we probably would not be in the place we are in and our vision and hope would not seem so far away.

But when deception is being used as a weapon against us; our vision seems cloudy and there is no certainty or absolutes. Anytime confusion is present, there seems to be a spirit of fear.

Where fear is present, there is usually doubt and unbelief. Where there is doubt and unbelief, our vision becomes weaker and weaker until it is totally lost.

PRAY IN THE SPIRIT

To regain our vision and get back on track with God, we have to overcome the wicked one. We cannot possibly do this in our own strength.

God is a Spirit. (John 4:24) When we need spiritual success, we must pray in the Spirit. Spiritual battles must be fought with spiritual weapons.

Our armed forces would not send men and women into battle without proper training and without the proper weapons. What good would it do to train our soldiers with weapons of war and then send them into battle without appropriate weapons to complete their task?

God does not expect his church to win the war against satan by battling in the flesh. The Word says we do not fight against flesh and blood. What we do fight against is spiritual wickedness in high places!

Ephesians 6: 12

"For we wrestle not against flesh and blood, but against principalities, against powers, against the rulers of the darkness of this world, against spiritual wickedness in high places".

These spirits know how to work through the fleshly bodies on earth by causing strife, division, and confusion. But most of the time when it comes to the flesh battling spiritual battles, we don't use good wisdom and spiritual technique. We begin by trying to manhandle spiritual issues as if we were handling something in the natural. We are fleshly bodies with a spiritual destiny. When it comes to battling spiritual battles, Apostle Paul tells us that we must pray in the Spirit if we are to win spiritual battles.

1 Corinthians 14:15 (NKJV)

"What is the conclusion then? I will pray with the spirit, and I will also pray with the understanding. I will sing with the spirit, and I will also sing with the understanding."

Apostle Paul gave the church some spiritual insight. When we pray we must pray with the Holy Spirit, but pray with understanding also. When we are losing our vision or have lost our vision, we must pray that the circumstances that are blinding our spiritual minds would be removed so that our vision is clear.

There are times when your vision is lost and you don't know what to pray. Sometimes when a person loses their vision they are so affected by doubt and unbelief they can't pray effectively. This is the time to press in and pray asking for spiritual help. We are to not only pray but pray *with* the Spirit. Again, Apostle Paul said in the book of Romans that there would be times when we don't know exactly what to pray, so we are to allow the Spirit of God within us to make intercession for us.

Romans 8:26

"Likewise the Spirit also helps in our weaknesses. For we do not know what we should pray for as we ought, but the Spirit Himself makes intercession for us according to God's will."

I don't know about you but when my spirit man is praying, I feel as though I am getting my breakthrough. Sometimes when I am praying and I am barely holding on with only a small measure of faith, it is hard for me to know what to pray. Therefore, I rely on my spirit man to make intercession for me. I believe when we don't know exactly what to pray, the Holy Ghost in us knows what we should pray.

People often ask me; when you pray, does God really hear our English or does it need to be translated spiritually? I believe as Adam walked and talked with God in the cool of the day, God understood Adam perfectly. I believe that whatever language a person may speak, God does not have a language barrier problem. Our Lord is the one who gave us the gifts and I have never seen or heard of a bad gift given from God. He does not give bad gifts to those who believe that He is God.

Luke 11:1

"If a son shall ask bread of any of you that is a father, will he give him a stone? or if he ask a fish, will he for a fish give him a serpent?"

James 1:17

"Every good gift and every perfect gift is from above, and comes down from the Father of lights, with whom there is no variation or shadow of turning."

THE PROMISES OF GOD

When loss of vision becomes a part of your life always fall back upon your promises and relationship of your God. God has always had a plan for His Church from the very beginning but it is up to the saints to believe His Word. For example, God's plan is for the believers to put action with His promises. If we are sick, we are to confess the words of healing. If we need finances, we are to confess the blessing of God upon us and over us. (Duet. 8:18) Therefore, by taking action upon His Word when we lose vision, we can have our promises restored in its fullness.

Remember that it is our own abilities that we doubt, not the Word.

Just recently I was asked to explain how our faith is activated within us to receive the things of God. Since He is spiritual and we are flesh we need revelation of how we can *"receive"*. One thing that we know is that our faith comes and is increased every time we put ourselves in the place of hearing His Word. Our minds must be renewed daily with the Word. Apostle Paul said in Romans 12 that if we allow our minds to be renewed, we could be transformed and separated from the ways of the world. Even though the Apostle said that faith comes by hearing and hearing the Word, we must activate the faith that we have within us in order that we might receive the promises of God.

How do we activate our faith? If it comes by hearing, (Romans 10:17) how do we keep it? One of the best ways to keep faith activated in our lives is to use your faith daily. Using our gift of faith pleases God. We are told without faith, it is impossible to please Him. (Heb. 11:6). But if we keep our faith activated and use our faith, then He is a rewarder of those who diligently seek Him.

How do we keep our faith? If the enemy can get you discouraged and secluded, then he is on his way to winning a victory. We have all gone this route before but let me explain.

> *There comes a time when our relationship with God has to become more important than our problems.*

Let us say that you have just come from a dynamic church service and was filled to overflowing by the Spirit of the Lord once again. Your minister preached a wonderful revelation that went straight to the heart. Wow! Don't you wish every Sunday was as fulfilling.

But now you are alone in your car and on your way out to eat *alone* because no one invited you to go with him or her. The enemy's plan is beginning to be set in place. The thoughts begin to come. *"They didn't want you to go along because you are so hard to talk to. You're always too religious. They really don't like you- you know. You are not liked very well".* Do you get the point? Little thoughts, if allowed, begin to seclude you. Suddenly, you find yourself getting angry. But angry with whom? Are you angry with your friends or the enemy? Keeping our faith focused in the right direction can sometimes be a challenge.

Doubt and unbelief will bring your faith to an all time low. Remember that it is our own abilities that we doubt, not the Word. The Word stands on its own with assurance. The Bible says if we fall upon the Word we will be broken, but if the Word falls on us, we will be ground to powder.

Though you are not responsible to perform your healing, it is a basic requirement that you initiate and activate your faith so that God's promise can be put into effect. It is a spiritual law that still exists today. If you don't activate your *faith*, you have not activated your hope. For *faith* is the substance, that brings your hope into a reality.

Hebrews 11:1

"Now faith is the substance of things hoped for, the evidence of things not seen."

Hebrews 11:6

"But without faith it is impossible to please him: for he that cometh to God must believe that he is, and that he is a rewarder of them that diligently seek him."

When you realize that your vision is lost, start asking the Lord to reveal truth. By activating your *faith* and *moving* in obedience, you have announced to the enemy that all doubt and unbelief has been removed and you are taking back your destiny. As believers, even when we lose sight of where we are, we must have *faith* in God. When everything seems to fall by the wayside, our belief in His Word must rise to the top and declare His goodness. Yes, even when our flesh doesn't want to. When you are in the midst of a dry season and there are no leaves *(fruit)* on the tree, we still must pray and maintain relationship with Jesus Christ. Most everyone will have a few bad hair days, but there comes a time when our relationship with God has to become more important than our problems. After all, it is life's *challenges* that the enemy magnifies to make our vision become dim. The enemy knows that if we become more focused on our problems rather than on God and destiny, then he has won a small victory until we come to our senses.

▶ PRAYER FOR RELEASE

Father, in the name of Jesus, I ask that you break from me the bondages and mindsets of the flesh. It is of my own free will that I pray for the blessings of the Word. I have lost vision because of doubt and unbelief. The enemy has tricked me in believing that I am not worthy of your vision, therefore I have believed a lie. I know that you love me, and I stand before you in repentance, believing in faith that all things will work together for good. I am a believer. I am saved. I have eternal life. And from this day forward, I will stand in faith, believing what the Word says I am. I do have the mind of Christ and I am worthy because of the blood of the Lamb.

I can do all things through Christ who strengthens me. In Him I live and move and have my being. Where the Spirit of the Lord is there is Liberty. I am free from bondages. Father, I ask by the measure of faith that you put in me, help me now. I release that helpless feeling that says I can't make it. Your Word says that I have already succeeded by the blood of the Lamb. I have already overcome. Therefore, I renew my vision right now by my faith in you. Thank you Lord. Amen

CHAPTER THREE

TRANSFORMATION

It is time that believers stop climbing mountains and become mountain movers! We were given all power and authority over the wicked one but it seems that we are constantly battling the same wars. Have you ever stopped to think that this could be happening because we are not moving? We have stationed ourselves around the bottom of our mountain and have only moved around enough to gain different scenery. We have become so familiar to the surroundings of where we were; we had to move to make ourselves feel better about ourselves. We get stuck in an "old" thing and become so comfortable that God has to literally dry up the brook so we will move again.

NEW LEVELS DURING DRY SEASONS

At one time or another we have all been at the brook Cherith like Elijah the Tishbite. Isn't it amazing how we can one day have all power and faith and the next day - doubt our own salvation? Our faith is similar to Elijah's. One day he is calling fire down from heaven and the next day he is running for his life. Does this experience relate or sound familiar? One day we leave our dynamic church service feeling like nothing could ever stop us from serving God with all power and might, and *suddenly* something hits your backspace memory button and you're taken back to an old thought. A *suddenly* can come because of something somebody said, or maybe a feeling, or perhaps because someone did not recognize you're talent or ability. *Suddenly* we find ourselves in a state of loneliness. And almost instantly we fall into what I refer to as a winter season. Winter seasons are mostly dry and everything seems to be dead to the natural eye. But remember that it is the winter seasons when there is no fruit on the tree that the root system grows deeper and deeper. It is the *process* that takes place *during* the winter season that allows our spiritual maturity to develop in strength and character. Even Elijah remained teachable during his winter season and listened for the Lord to speak and give direction.

It is these dry winter places that make it the hardest to stand firm. But it is those seasons of dryness when we gain the most spiritual knowledge. It seems that the "winter seasons" are the most beneficial because we are moved to the next level. I have noticed that I receive more revelation when I am challenged the most. Winter seasons force us out of our comfortable habitant so that God can extract our hidden potential. God is always trying to promote us, but as He begins to transform us we get overwhelmed by the slightest tug. This is why we must lay hold to His promises and believe He will perfect everything concerning us.

Psalm 18:32

"It is God that girdeth me with strength, and maketh my way perfect."

When God begins his purification process and starts extracting our potential, *everything* becomes exposed. The Spirit of the Lord touches the hidden areas that man hides from society. The Holy Spirit never overlooks the hidden areas that we think are covered up. We might think that just because our Pastor or church friends or relatives don't see the ugly stuff, everything will be all right. The Bible tells us that God knows the thoughts and intent of our hearts before we even know them. He even knows what we think before we ask. If the Lord knows every hair on our head and our thoughts, as well as actions, we must have enough knowledge to realize that God is a lot smarter than mankind. His ways are higher than our ways and His thoughts are higher than our thoughts. (Isaiah 55:8-9)

Somehow lifestyles of today seem to override the intentions of man's hearts. As believers in Christ, Christians harden their hearts to sin and continue their daily activities. They go to ungodly movies, seek adult entertainment, but yet call themselves Christians. All the while they go to church and continue to entangle themselves in sin and go through life as if nothing has happened. I don't know if you have noticed or not, but the church has stopped calling sin - sin. When someone has sinned, it is differed to as a problem. It is not only a problem, but it is a *sin* against God!

> *It is the process that takes place during the winter season that allows our spiritual maturity to develop in strength and character.*

It is not uncommon for the ugliness of our hearts to be exposed during winter seasons. God begins to tug on our hearts and suddenly we begin to lose our vision. Suddenly something has changed from the normal way of doing things. We think this is not the way I planned it. I must be in transition! Change? I don't like change! Your comfort zone is now being challenged. You feel out of place and out of control. You will feel as if you don't belong. Your vision has become cloudy. You're not seeing clearly any longer. The very thing that used to give you life is now of no importance to you. The axe is being laid to the root. Your focus has changed.

During this purification process your vision can be easily lost if your focus is not clear. Remember one thing, stay <u>focused</u> or you will totally lose vision.

God has not left you; He is only taking you to a level you do not recognize. Most people fall into a category of rejection and abandonment during this time. They often feel that they are unloved and unwanted when this happens. It is not that you or anyone around you has changed; it is your *circumstances* that are changing. You are still you. You have not lost your salvation. God is still with you. But you have never been this way before. God is only narrowing and perfecting your pathway. But before He can allow you to go forth and be trusted with much, you must be faithful with little. To whom much is given, much is required.

> *God is only narrowing and perfecting your pathway.*

I asked the Lord years ago why it seemed so hard when the Lord begin strengthening our tent stakes. He revealed to me the hardness in a way that I understood. The Holy Spirit said it was like going on a vacation in the mountains but you forgot to dress for the occasion. At first this made no sense to me, but then I began to put the thoughts together. If I were going to the mountains, and in order to be comfortable, I would need to take certain clothes, boots, and camping equipment.

When the Lord moves us to a new level, he allows us to get there even though we are not dressed for the occasion. Usually maturity, wisdom, character, and stability is achieved *after* we arrive. God is good at equipping the called. You may even feel as if you are not ready for this level, but we do not lean to our own understanding. It is God that is bringing the promotion and not man.

Psalm 75:6-7

6 *"For promotion cometh neither from the east, nor from the west, nor from the south.*

7 *But God is the judge: he putteth down one, and setteth up another."*

When transformation begins its process, *(and there is always a process)* there are several thoughts that come to mind. I cannot possibly list all that one might think but here are a few.

1. Am I willing to go through the process?
2. Am I strong enough to go into a process of change?
3. Does God really want me to change?
4. Why do I have to change?
5. I don't see everybody else changing!

BE WILLING TO CHANGE

I have come to the conclusion that we must be willing to change in order to reach our destiny. Abraham was willing to sojourn the land even though he did not know where he was going. He knew his relationship with God was coupled with the promises of God. Abraham knew that his promises were already waiting on him before he experienced the breakthrough. Even though he did not know how or when these would manifest, he had faith in God and God counted his faith righteousness. Abraham's faith had to be heart faith because he came from a background of idol worshippers. That is why the Lord had to move him away from his family and friends in Ur. Abraham did not receive his promises until he was obedient to step out from an old place. We speak our salvation by our mouth, but it is our heart that we believe unto righteousness.

Romans 10:9-10

9 *"That if thou shalt confess with thy mouth the Lord Jesus, and shalt believe in thine heart that God hath raised him from the dead, thou shalt be saved.*

10 *For with the heart man believeth unto righteousness; and with the mouth confession is made unto salvation."*

We cannot afford to rest in the anointing that God gives us and not be willing to change. If Abraham would have been unwilling to endure the process of transformation by leaving his family (Gen. 12) I believe that God would have chosen someone else. God's plan for his church had already been predestined and His Word will come to pass. God's promises for HIS church have been manifested from generation to generation.

The book of Ephesians tells us in Chapter One that before the foundation of the world the church was known. So if God foreknew the church of today, we too must be as Abraham and hold on to our promises before we experience them. Our transformation can only come when we are willing to be obedient and follow the Spirit of the Lord.

If the widow woman in Elijah's time (who had nothing), was unwilling to change, she would have continued in her *self*-made destiny and would have probably starved to death. But God not only had a plan for Elijah but also had a plan in Zarephath for the widow woman.

Even though Elijah's provision had been previously promised to him, he still had to walk through the process of having no water or food until he reached his destination.

So it is with our transformation process. We sometimes expect God to move upon our situation immediately and remove our burdens. From the beginning of time, I believe that God's perfect plan for Adam was that he was never to experience pain. He was to tend His garden, be fruitful and multiply and live happily ever after. However, when man disobeyed God, allowing the rebellion to come into the heart, God ordered man to plant his own seed and toil the ground for his provision. Remember it was Eve that was deceived, but Adam simply disobeyed. Disobedience is as the same as witchcraft (I Samuel 15:23). Therefore, God was furious with Adam and Eve and ejected them from the garden.

God is so wise and skillful when it comes to transforming. In the beginning of time He transformed darkness into light, a barren land into fruitfulness, and established everything to reproduce after its own kind. Yet we, as believers, get lost in the process of transformation because of our unwillingness to participate. It's not the transformation and fruitfulness of God alone, but God through man and man through God. Meaning, what we sow is what we reap. The Lord gave us His Word that every seed shall bear fruit after its own kind. (Genesis 1:11)

Therefore, if a transformation process is to manifest in our lives, we must take the necessary steps and be *willing* for fruitfulness to occur. It is we who must take the first step to show God that we mean business.

We cannot be transformed until our minds are renewed. Apostle Paul said it best in the book of Romans Chapter Twelve when he stated that the renewing of our minds must take place <u>first</u>. Without our minds being renewed from the *"old things"* we would fall back into the same old mindsets, therefore, losing our victory. It is our minds that play the vital part in our transformation success. Our flesh does not receive spiritual understanding and will never understand the supernatural things.

1 Corinthians 2:14

"But the natural man does not receive the things of the Spirit of God, for they are foolishness to him; nor can he know them, because they are spiritually discerned."

Apostle Paul had changed his way of thinking from having a worldly point of view into having Godly spiritual understanding. His road to Damascus experience in Acts Nine was only to bring about a transformation from a Saul to a Paul. His lifestyle had to change. His thoughts had to change. Everything about him had to change. Paul could no longer give thought to the things of old. His ways had to become totally different. He could not allow his new transformation to become tainted with the things of his past. His will to change could not be stopped. His vision was to take on the things of the Lord and press toward the prize of the high calling.

> *Abraham did not receive his promises until he was obedient to step out from an old place.*

CAUGHT IN THE MIDDLE

Have you ever wondered why the Lord had to bring blindness upon Paul in order to get him to a place of spiritual understanding? I asked the Lord about Paul's blindness and the Spirit of the Lord spoke this to me:

"If I allowed him to look back in his own eyes, he would only see his successes according to his flesh. I had to show Paul that his successes could not be measured with my spiritual successes because my ways are higher. His way of thinking had to be totally transformed. So I blinded him temporarily in the natural to allow Paul to be led by the Spirit for the first time. From this point forward, if he was to see the miraculous things of God, they had to be seen in the Spirit first and then manifested in the natural. Paul had to begin to believe and have faith in me, that all things are possible, even his restoration of his natural eyesight. I enabled Paul to see in the Spirit first and then know in his natural mind by faith that whatever he had faith for, that too would come to pass."

> We cannot afford to rest in the anointing that God gives us and not be willing to change.

Little did Paul know that his mental process would be so transformed. His way of seeing things from the natural to the spiritual would change his life and his ministry, which would be exemplified for thousands of years to come. Paul's experiences would lay many foundations for Sunday morning church services around the world.

Just as Jesus was in the tomb for three days, so it was with Paul being blinded. It was a dark place for Paul. While experiencing blindness for three days he had no choice but to walk by faith and pray for the restoration natural sight. Just as Paul was led blindly to his new destination, so it is with our transformation. We can only expect a total renewing of our Spirit man if we trust in the Lord with all our hearts and understanding. Like Apostle Paul, Abraham, or King David of old, before we can reach our mount Zion, *Gods dwelling place*, we too must climb our mountain.

John 20:29

".... Blessed are those who have never seen, yet believe."

When you are in transition, you seem to be right in the middle of things. You are not out of the old completely but you're not totally in the new either. It is kind of like being a teenager. You are not totally into adulthood but you're not a child anymore.

It is like going to school all over again. You just finished high school but there is more to learn. You go to college and you are looking for that new job but employers dictate the need for experience. You graduate and move from having no knowledge of a subject to receiving a degree in a particular subject. But just because you have passed all the exams on paper doesn't mean a company has need of your wisdom.

Apostle Paul had to let go of the old things in order for the new to be accomplished. The new can never manifest while cleaving to the old. Expansion can never come if there is no room for its expression. Apostle Paul's Damascus road experiences demanded knowledge that he did not have before. Without that particular experience, Paul would have never experienced destiny.

TRANSFORMATION IS A GOOD THING

When the Lord is doing your transforming, there is little you can do to change the circumstances. After all, would you really want to change what the Lord has predestined? Our flesh would cry out yes; but the spirit man knows that those who are led by the Spirit of God are the Sons of God. (Romans 8:14). Too often we bail out of the presence of God because our transformation process is too difficult. But just as Samuel had to let go of Saul and fill his own horn with fresh oil, we too must step into our present anointing so the Lord can mature us into destiny. Like sanctification, we must release the old in order to manifest our newness. Jesus can only pour in the new wine if we are willing to become flexible allowing our wineskins to embrace the new wine. We know that old wine skins are not flexible therefore oil must be rubbed and massaged into the old skin until flexibility comes. Just as the Lord saw Paul as his chosen vessel to bear HIS name before the Gentiles, kings, and Israelites (Acts 9:15), so it is that the Lord has chosen you and I. We are also to go before the nonbelievers and confess Jesus as the Savior and Lord of this world. Transformation can be a good thing if we are willing to go through the process.

FIRST THINGS FIRST

Remember, God does not always call the qualified, but He always qualifies the called. He is more interested in you being transformed into His likeness, than you being transformed to be in the ministry. Man seems to always get it backwards. We cry out for the Lord to impart His ministry into us, but are not willing to go through transformation. We want to preach the gospel in the entire world but are not willing to take care of Jerusalem first. Before we are able to go to the uttermost parts of the world, we first must conquer our Jerusalem, meaning our back yards first. Sometimes our vision is so large we start somewhere else because it is easier to be somewhere else other than where we need to be. Our Lord knows what we are capable of, but sometimes we have more zeal than wisdom. Apostle Peter was willing to build three tabernacles on the mount of transfiguration but Father God interrupted Peter and asks Peter to just be quiet and listen unto His Son whom He was well pleased. All of a sudden when Father God showed up, everyone fell on their knees and listened.

We too are guilty of getting ahead of God. There have been many ministries launched but have not been *"called"*. It is true that God equips whom He calls but first things first. There is much to be said about good healthy counseling. Not only when visions are lost or your marriage is falling apart, but good counseling is healthy when you need to make a quality decision.

Proverbs 11:14

"Where no counsel is, the people fall: but in the multitude of counsellers there is safety."

Counseling is what we need sometimes during transformation. We need to call upon people of wisdom and listen to the Holy Spirit who will bring us comfort during our times of making decisions. There are times when a person needs to be alone in their prayer closet and get their own answers from God, but there are definite times of counsel as well. Especially when you have lost vision and hope and are not able to hear the Lord's direction.

SIZING UP YOUR CIRCUMSTANCES

One of the ways we know if the transforming is being done by the Father is to size up your circumstances. If you are in the middle of a dry season, a storm, or in a process of transformation, you must stop and spiritually discern what is taking place. If you are being stripped from every direction but there is no provision, then you are being tested by the enemy. When you are being tested of the enemy, usually there is no provision during the testing. When God brings forth a purging process there is always provision. When Elijah was being purged, even though he thought he was alone, God provided food and water.

> *Too often we bail out of the presence of God because our transformation process is too difficult.*

When Jonah was thrown overboard to drown, God provided a vessel to take him to dry land. So when you are feeling alone and deserted, check the circumstances to see if there is provision. Even though the children of Israel wondered in the wilderness for forty years, their sandals never wore out, their food supply seem to always be there, their clothes never wore out, and/or God always provided a source for them to make new ones. Being transformed can take on a whole new meaning when we understand the ways of our Lord. Transformation will take you to a new level in the Spirit each time God does the purging. But there is another thing you should know. God always does a purging before a new level can be achieved. And at each new level there is always a purging. Don't jump ship or leave your river too quickly, before the provision runs out.

> *Transformation will take you to a new level in the Spirit each time God does the purging.*

Remember the Lord will always meet your need not your greed.

▶ PRAYER FOR TRANSFORMATION

Father God I thank you for being my strength and my provider. There are times when I feel as if I am being torn in every direction. But I know that you are instilling good things in me. Cleanse me from all unrighteousness and put a clean heart in me. I want what you want. Even though I try to jump ship when things get rough, don't let me bypass my hour of opportunity. When storms are rocking my boat, I pray that you will always be in my boat. Don't let me sink now Lord! Lord it is hard to go through purification. But as long as You are doing the purging, I am willing to stand the fire. Help me during the transforming process to hold on to the vision. Without vision I could perish. Lord, you are the life giver. You are Jehovah Jireh my provider. You are Jehovah Shalom, the God of peace. Help me to have provision and peace during this process of transformation. Amen.

CHAPTER FOUR

THE SPIRIT OF DEATH

It is an awful feeling when you have lost your vision. When vision dies there comes a hopelessness upon you and loneliness prevails. When it's gone, the very thing that was shining the brightest in your life is now only an empty space that needs filling. It is not that you are giving up; it is the enemy working overtime to bring discouragement and hopelessness, robbing you of your destiny.

Colossians 1: 27-28 (KJV)

27 *"Even the mystery which hath been hid from ages and from generations, but <u>now</u> is made manifest to his saints:*

28 *To whom God would make known what is riches of the glory of this mystery among the Gentiles; which is Christ in you, the **hope** of glory."*

Your vision has not changed, but your thoughts are being overshadowed. The spirit that is bringing death to your vision has found a way to distract you from the very thing that is giving you fulfillment. The spirit of death is now placing obstacles in your way to block your vision. Its purpose is to squeeze all life from its victims and separate them from anything that supplies life.

Apostle Paul writes of the patriarch Abraham and says in the book of Romans 4: 18,20;

18 *"Who against hope believed in hope, that he might become the father of many nations; according to that which was spoken...*

20 *He staggered not at the promise of God through unbelief; but was strong in faith, giving glory to GOD."*

Isn't it amazing that Abraham was able to push through just by hanging on to a substance that he could not see? Our faith has to become a power source when our hope is deferred. Abraham had to be fully persuaded by his faith in God that regardless of what may come his way, he was still able to press beyond his soulish reasoning. His faith had to be at a level of not allowing the spirit of death to take away his promises from the Lord.

The enemy comes to snatch away our vision and tries to steal our faith in God by suggesting vain imaginations. He tempts our thoughts with doubt and unbelief. He strongly urges us to believe the same lie as Eve believed saying, *"Hath God said?"*

Apostle Paul declares that we are to cast down imaginations and bind the thoughts of our mind and hold them captive.

II Corinthians 10:5

"Casting down imaginations and every high thing that exalts itself against the knowledge of God, and bring into captivity every thought to the obedience of Christ".

When we come into agreement with his seductive lies, it affects our bodies. Our bodies begin to align with the lies we've believed. Everything that our bodies do is filtered through our minds. Therefore, the enemy knows that if he can get us to dwell on thoughts of being suicidal or becoming self destructive, he has set us up for failure. The enemy has not only unloosed a spirit of murder upon our lives, but has made a direct attack against God Himself.

How can this be you might ask? Why is it that the enemy is always attacking us personally?

It is because we are the temple of God and are bought with the blood of Jesus.

1 Corinthians 3:16

"Know ye not that ye are the temple of God, and that the Spirit of God dwelleth in you?"

Jesus did not suffer and die upon a wooden cross for the enemy to have authority upon this earth. We, the Church, have been given all authority over every evil work and the enemy has been sent to this earth for the Church to torture! However, we must not forget that just because we are blood bought, we can still be tempted. If Jesus was tempted, and He was, so shall we be tempted. But remember, even though temptations come, we have overcome.

> *Our faith has to become a power source when our hope is deferred.*

Revelation 12:11

"And they <u>overcame</u> him by the blood of the Lamb, and by the word of their testimony; and they loved not their lives unto the death."

SPIRITUAL WARFARE

There are seasons in our lives when the enemy fights harder than at other times. Some of you who are reading this may not understand spiritual warfare. Please allow me to explain this briefly.

Spiritual warfare is a term that is not taught in most fundamentalist churches, or at least it wasn't taught in mine. Therefore, when I began to study to show myself approved, it did not take me long to find out that I had been fighting battles all along; only now I was beginning to understand <u>what</u> I was fighting. I have realized the enemy comes in a disguise as long as he can get away with it. But by the gift of discerning of spirits (I Cor. 12: 10) we are able to identify spiritual attacks of the wicked one. Discernment is a gift from God that reveals which evil spirit we are dealing with.

It is also important for us to remember that when we are in *spiritual* warfare we are battling a *spirit*. And when we battle a spiritual battle in the flesh we can easily be worn out.

Daniel 7:25

"And he shall speak great words against the most High, and shall wear out the saints of the most High, and think to change times and laws: and they shall be given into his hand until a time and times and the dividing of time."

The Apostle tells us in scripture that even though we walk in the flesh, we do not war after the flesh.

2 Corinthians 10:3

"For though we walk in the flesh, we do not war after the flesh:"

This previous passage means that our flesh cannot enter into a spiritual battle. Paul tells us in the book of First Corinthians chapter two and verse fourteen, that the natural man receives not the things of the Spirit of God; for they are foolishness unto him; neither can he know them, because they are spiritually discerned.

In spiritual warfare you must use the "power of choice".

1 Corinthians 2:14

"But the natural man receiveth not the things of the Spirit of God: for they are foolishness unto him: neither can he know them, because they are spiritually discerned."

When we are to engage in a spiritual battle, our flesh is not effective. Because we have the Spirit of God within us, we must call upon our spiritual man to do the work for us.

I use the words *"when we engage"* because the Christ has given every believer power over the forces of hell. Therefore, I believe that we can choose our battles. In spiritual warfare you must use the *"power of choice"*. The power of choice means that since you have been given all authority over the wicked one, that it is you who chooses the battleground.

Luke 10:19

"Behold, I give unto you power to tread on serpents and scorpions, and over all the power of the enemy: and nothing shall by any means hurt you."

If you are dealing with other problems in you life, then don't walk onto another battleground. Remember, the blood of Christ has purchased your victories and you fight *from* the victory and not *to* the victory.

There are some Christians that war in the flesh and find themselves tired and worn out. It is because the natural body cannot war a spiritual battle! Yes we go to battle, but it is our spirit man that must do the engaging. I have witnessed saint's binding and loosing, yelling, declaring, and wearing their flesh out hoping that all their emotions are effective. I am not against demonstration. There are several demonstrations of the *"arts"* such as mime and dance that illustrate waging war against the enemy.

The Bible speaks about clapping, dancing, shouting, and the playing of instruments that will silence the enemy.

Psalm 47

"O clap your hands, all ye people; shout unto God with the voice of triumph."

Psalm 149:3-7

3 *"Let them praise his name in the dance: let them sing praises unto him with the timbrel and harp.*

4 *For the LORD taketh pleasure in his people: he will beautify the meek with salvation.*

5 Let the saints be joyful in glory: let them sing aloud upon their beds.

6 Let the high praises of God be in their mouth, and a two edged sword in their hand;"

I am referring to people who go through the natural motions when others are around just to look spiritual. Demonstration without proper application and revelation does not affect the camp of the enemy. But when corporate faith is added to orderly demonstration during a time of Holy Ghost direction, it becomes a destructive tool against the forces of hell.

The Pharisee's would not pray in secret, instead they prayed so everyone could conclude they were spiritual. When Jesus taught his disciples, He told them not to pray as the Pharisee's but rather pray in secret and their rewards would be openly. I pray that no religious spirits would misinterpret what I am trying to convey here, because there are times to do demonstration warfare and there are times to pray in our prayer closets. However, as believers we are not to exhaust our energy's before every service and come into the sanctuary's sweating so that people can see how religious we are.

CORPORATE ANOINTINGS

I have noticed over the years that when God pours out His anointing for warfare corporately, the whole congregation enters into warfare. When God does this it is just not one or two that is into demonstration.

Every church should be sensitive to the Spirit of the Lord and follow His spiritual direction. When the Holy Spirit says to war, the church should go through acts of declaring war. When the Spirit says to be silent and know that He is God, then we should allow the Holy Spirit to move in His greatness.

Too often the body of Christ is quick to jump into a time of quietness with a Word of the Lord, Word of Knowledge, or an act of demonstration, instead of being still and listening for a small still voice. There are times to be silent, times to prophesy, times to war, and times to worship. But these acts should be carried out under the guidelines of the local governmental Church and their authority. Every saint, when they become a member of a local church, comes under the accountability of that particular corporate anointing.

> Demonstration without proper application and revelation does not affect the camp of the enemy.

There is so much to be said about spiritual warfare and warfare praise. But in order to bring a conclusion to this subject, let me say that we will always have trials, battles, and spiritual attacks while in our mortal bodies. However, because of the precious blood of our Lord Jesus we are enabled to fight <u>from</u> the victory and not <u>to</u> the victory. This means that the battle has already been won for every believer and in faith we know we are already victorious before we go to battle!

I felt it was necessary to briefly discuss spiritual warfare because many people lose their vision during episodes of spiritual conflict. As mature believers we must focus our thoughts not upon the problem but fix our thoughts upon the Word of God. We must believe in the report of the Lord which says, I am healed, I am free, I have the mind of Christ, I have overcome, I have been blood bought, I have Christ within me, I am the temple of God, I can do all things through Christ my Lord! Like Caleb, we are to have a good report.

Thus far we have discussed the spirit of death that attacks vision and a spiritual death. Let us now take a look at the natural spirit of death that comes to steal life from a living soul. Once again this is spiritual warfare.

It is only by the blood of the Lamb that we can defeat the *"spirit of death"*. Just as the Israelites found themselves obeying the Word of the Lord, so we too must obey the Lord. In Exodus chapter twelve they were instructed to kill a lamb and place the blood on their doorpost so that the spirit of death would pass by their house; so it is with our battle with the enemy. We too put the blood of Christ over the doorposts of our hearts. The blood of Christ is the only power over the spirit of death because only the blood contains redemptive power.

In Exodus we see the Lord dispatching the spirit of death to all the first born children and the first born of the animals. The Lords purpose was to bring freedom to the Israelites. The key to freedom was the blood of a lamb. We must never underestimate the power of the blood.

Exodus 12:29

"And it came to pass, that at midnight the Lord smote all the firstborn in the land of Egypt, from the firstborn of Pharaoh that sat on his throne unto the firstborn of the captive that was in the dungeon; and all the firstborn of cattle."

The Lord gave the Israelites a key to surpass the spirit of death. As they applied the blood, death's power was neutralized and life was maintained. It was by obedience and faith that they applied the blood over the doorpost and survived. This key still works today. When we by faith apply the blood of the lamb (Jesus) over the doorposts of our hearts, that same enemy must pass by and not harm us in any way.

I believe that if an Egyptian had been standing behind a door that had the blood of a lamb upon it, the spirit of death would have still passed over that door as well.

Exodus 12:7, 13

7 *"And they shall take of the blood, and strike it on the two side posts and on the upper doorpost of the houses, where they will be eating of the Lamb.*

13 *And the blood shall be to you for a token upon the houses where ye are: and when I see the blood, I will pass over you and the plague shall not be upon you, when I smite the land of Egypt."*

LEARNING THE ENEMY'S TACTICS

By understanding that the enemy's plan is to steal, kill, and destroy God's plan for you, (John 10:10) we must seek to read the plan of the enemy backwards. If the Lord used the spirit of death to bring freedom to the Israelites, then the enemy's plan is to bring death to your vision and stop you from pursuing your destiny.

Of coarse we don't want to stop pursuing our vision but the plan of the enemy is to get our thoughts to come into agreement with his plan. Your vision is the first thing that has to be in operation in order for you to accomplish your day. Your vision is the very tool that keeps you on track. Where there is no vision, people perish! (Proverbs 29:18)

The enemy always seems to use the tactics of God but never able to equal HIS character. The spirit of death can only be used as a tactic of the enemy. The reason it can only be a tactic and not a fact, is that it was the blood of a lamb that made the spirit of death pass over the doors of families. The blood of Christ is as effective today as the blood of an animal was in that day. We simply confess Christ as Savior and Lord and instantly we are covered by His redemptive blood.

Remember this when death knocks on your door. The blood of Jesus Christ who died for our sins, sickness, and diseases has shed HIS blood once and forever. Jesus has overcome death, hell, and the grave; therefore, the spirit of death cannot come neigh your dwelling. If the enemy comes as a spirit of death, remember that the blood of Christ has covered your life. Like the old song goes I learned as a child, "What can wash away my sin? Nothing but the <u>blood</u> of Jesus. What can make me whole again? Nothing but the <u>blood</u> of Jesus."

Hebrews 9:12

'Neither by the blood of goats and calves, but by His own blood he entered in once into the holy place, having obtained eternal redemption for us.'

When you receive revelation of the power of the blood, the forces of hell have to move back and mountains removed.

Mark 11:22-24

22 *"And Jesus answering saith unto them, Have faith in God.*

23 *For verily I say unto you, That whosoever shall say unto this mountain, Be thou removed, and be thou cast into the sea; and shall not doubt in his heart, but shall believe that those things which he saith shall come to pass; he shall have whatsoever he saith*

24 *Therefore I say unto you, What things soever ye desire, when ye pray, believe that ye receive them, and ye shall have them."*

OPENING DOORS TO CURSES

The spirit of death usually finds a place of habitation when a vessel becomes weakened and has opened a door for spiritual attack. A suicidal person or persons suffering with low self-esteem are prime candidates. It is possible that a person who becomes a victim of this particular spirit is not responsible for their actions. Let me explain.

A person who has generational curses may become a victim of the spirit of death. Generational curses can be passed down through the years and because of *"lack of knowledge"* we are constantly being attacked. (Hosea 4:6) We must educate ourselves in this area that doors can be closed from passed curses. By knowing the history of our great grandfathers and great grandmothers and others in the generational lineage, we can sometimes pinpoint the spirit that is causing the havoc. This is not to say that the curses started with them, but if open doors are not closed generationally to the curses, they will continue to exist.

> *Jesus has overcome death, hell, and the grave; therefore, the spirit of death cannot come neigh your dwelling.*

It could be that the spirit of death that was not successful in their father, grandfather, great grandfather, or perhaps on their mother's side as well, is still present trying to find a family member that is a carrier of the spirit of death. The Word of God says that generational spirits of iniquity and transgression and sin, can visit the children of the fathers and upon the children's children unto the third and to the fourth generation.

Exodus 34: 7

Keeping mercy for thousands, forgiving iniquity and transgression and sin, and will by no means clear the guilty; visiting the iniquity of the fathers upon the children and upon the children's children, unto the third and to the fourth generation.

This spirit is a nasty/ugly spirit that preys on the any vessel that opens the door.

By opening a door, I mean perhaps somewhere during a person's life they sinned and this allowed a curse to come upon the family. Let me explain.

If a curse is given a stronghold in a family by a family member contemplating suicide, it will stay with that family until someone of spiritual strength rises up and uses the Word of God and the power of the blood of Jesus and breaks the power of the curse.

I realize that some believe that a Christian cannot have a demonic curse but I have seen born again believers deal with terrible strongholds. Some may call it fleshly desires but after they received a measure of deliverance they become free from spiritual strongholds. The enemy is no respecter of persons.

LEGALIZED ABORTION

The Church of the 21st Century is living in a society with no respect for human life. The law of the land has given the spirit of death a legal right to exist. Our unborn babies are murdered before they have a chance to take their first breath. Our government is fully enforcing the Roe vs. Wade decision by every measure of legality. Our court system is fading into a new world order. Many present leaders of America are compromising the very freedom that was written by their forefathers hundreds of years ago. How long will the churches of tomorrow hold fast to the compromise of today? The spirit of darkness and death are upon the households of the world. We as believers are allowing this spirit to exist by avoiding confrontations with the enemy. Some non-profit organizations today don't even believe that we have a spiritual enemy. Some don't realize they have made silent covenants with the forces of hell. What kind of covenant you might ask? Perhaps one type of covenant would be this, *"Devil, you don't bother me, and I won't bother you"*.

Thousands of Christians have made this covenant vow with the enemy and have never rebuked the powers of darkness. I don't think that we need to look for demons in every dark corner, but it wouldn't hurt to send the Word of power toward every dark corner! Dr. Luke wrote in his first book and said to give light to those who sit in darkness and in the shadows of death. (Luke 1:79) We can no longer allow such wickedness to dominate our churches and homes in America.

The spirit of death is only one stronghold that has been discussed but believe me, there are several other spirits lurking in darkness waiting to manifest. Plead the blood of Jesus over your children and family. Declare that the spirits of darkness will not be able to penetrate or succeed in accomplishing their task. Having done all stand, stand ye therefore, and see the salvation of your GOD by taking the whole Armour of God. (Ephesians 6: 11-17)

CHAPTER REVIEW

In summary, let us quickly review some of the main topics of this chapter because there were basically three topics discussed, the spirit of death, warfare, and the redemptive blood of Christ.

When the spirit of death seems to be the main attack on your vision there will certainly be no life. You will feel like giving up, and hopelessness will occur in your thoughts, over and over and over. And probably the most devastating spirit that accompanies the spirit of death is the spirit of suicide.

> As we plead the blood, declaring that the spirit of death cannot come neigh our dwelling, we are declaring warfare.

When dealing with a suicidal stronghold, remember that the enemy is taking this attack much farther than just loss of vision. Loss of vision is losing hope or purpose to continue your destiny, but when the spirit of death comes, it is not trying simply to steal your vision; it is attempting to take your life!

Spirits of wickedness causes a person to become very confused and therefore their hope for living becomes saturated with a multitude of other problem areas. The weighted pressures of shame, guilt, confusion, and hopelessness are enough for our minds to only think on negative thoughts. Our mind feels as if it would be easier to die than to live. Don't believe the deceiver. Recall the Word and declare that your mind is the mind of Christ. For He has not given you the spirit of fear but love, power, and a sound mind. (II Timothy 1:7) Since fear is the opposite of faith, this is only an attack upon your mind.

Secondly, read the enemies mail backward. If he wants to take you out, then you must be doing something right. But if you dwell in self-pity and concentrate on the negative, then you will only empower the negative forces. That is why it is so important for us to recognize the spiritual attacks. The spirit of death will quickly retreat as you begin to plead the blood of Jesus over your mind and you repent of your negativity.

It is only the blood of Jesus that can set you free from the stronghold of the enemy. Just as the Israelites spread the lamb's blood over their doorposts when the spirit of death came, so it is with the spiritual blood of Christ that we plead with our words. Remember the power of God's Word. (Hebrews 4:12) *"It is sharper than a two edged sword and is quick and powerful and pierces even to the dividing asunder of soul and spirit, and of the joints and marrow, and is a discerner of the thoughts and intents of the heart."*

As we plead the blood, declaring that the spirit of death cannot come neigh our dwelling, we are declaring warfare. The enemy recognizes he was defeated by the blood of Jesus. It was the blood that bought you and I. Therefore, when the blood is declared by a covenant declaration of faith, the enemy cannot stand. Every word that proceeds out of your mouth can set you free. Just as every word that is spoken out of your mouth can bring bondage. It is not God's purpose that we be imprisoned by the works of the enemy, but just the opposite. We are to be free.

I John 3:8 says:

"He that committeth sin is of the devil; for the devil sinneth from the beginning. For this purpose the Son of God was manifested, that he might destroy the works of the devil".

Proverbs 18:21

"Death and life are in the power of the tongue."

Proverbs 21:23

"Whoso keepeth his mouth and his tongue keepeth his soul from trouble".

We do not fight to the victory but from the victory because Christ has already won the battle.

DECLARE WAR!

And thirdly, we must declare war on the enemy if we are to have spiritual success. Jesus died that we might destroy the wicked one, and has given the Church (us) the power to become victorious.

Spiritual warfare has to become part of our daily lives if we are to possess our inheritance through Jesus Christ by faith. (Gal. 3:14). Some believe that we can *"just hang on long enough"* until Jesus comes, we will be resurrected from earth and the enemy can't touch us any more.

But the Bible says that Jesus has already given us *all* power and the very authority that Jesus had, He has given it to us, the believer. (Luke 10:19)

So *warfare* is not something that we can avoid, but rather that we enter into it knowing that we have already won the victory. We do not fight to the victory but <u>from</u> the victory because Christ has already won the battle. We have nothing to fear, nothing to back down from, even when battling a spirit of death. It is the blood that puts us in right standing on all counts. It is not by our own strength or power, but the blood of Jesus that sets us free.

Zechariah 4:6

*"Then he answered and spake unto me, saying, This is the word of the LORD unto Zerubbabel, saying, Not by **might**, nor by **power**, but by My **Spirit**, saith the LORD of hosts".*

▶ Prayer of Deliverance

Father God, in Jesus name I repent right now for ever allowing my spirit to come into agreement with any spirit other than Yours. You are my Savior and Lord. I forsake and rebuke every other god that I have knowingly and unknowingly allowed to come into Your temple (this body). I confess You as Father God the supreme ruler of the universe. I believe that You loved me so much that You sent Your only begotten Son and He died for my transgressions. Jesus Christ went to the heart of the earth and took the keys from the Devil and the enemy has been stripped of his power. Jesus is now sitting beside the Father in the heavens and has given the Church the authority to carry out His mission. Jesus gave the keys to whosoever believes in the Son of God and confesses that Jesus is the Christ. Since I am a believer in Christ Jesus, no weapon formed against me shall prosper. I rebuke the spirit of death by the blood of the Lamb. Jesus Christ has stripped the enemy of his power; therefore my generation is cleared from the spirit of death. Devil you have no power in me or my family from this time forward. In the name of Jesus I pray. Amen!

CHAPTER FIVE

PROGRESS VERSES PROCESS

Most people hate the fact that everything we seem to obtain costs something. It is true, that when something of value is worth partaking of, it comes with a price. Our maturity in character and spirituality comes because God cares enough about us to walk us through a process. We want to rush through the journeys and get them over with, but God seems to have a way of slowing us down so that we can learn from every experience. It seems that God is in the marinating business and not in microwave business. So when our process comes, we must learn from our endeavors and experiences rather than focusing on the timing. Many times there is a death to a season and not the vision. If not discerned properly, one might assume that their vision has died, when actually it is only the season that has vanished.

God wants us to have **progress** in the natural and the spirit. But I have found that we gain *progress* only through process after process. In fact, it is the process that perfects your progress. Our experiences with God are what elevate us to a higher spiritual level. It is not our profound wisdom that skyrockets us to another spiritual high. It is only by His grace and power that we have the strength to endure another procedure. Just because we go thorough one process, does not equip us to handle all things.

It is not until we have completed task after task that we are able to gain wisdom and understanding.

It is not how many laps we can run or the number of circumstances we go through, but the challenge is, "Can we finish the race"? Even though our flesh rebels during a learning curve, God still requires us to be steadfast and to have sheer determination.

Some call each process a trial or an attack of the enemy. But if the maturing level is God doing the maturing, the challenge is only a battle against our flesh and not an attack of the enemy. God is having His way with His temple and our flesh is rebelling.

SPIRITUAL BIRTHING

When the Lord brings a believer to a new level we enter into what is known as a new birthing stage. Birthing stages are not easy but the final result is very exciting. Like having a newborn in your family can be very exciting in the natural, it can be equally exciting in the spiritual sense. But during the time of the birthing it is the mother that has to deal with the morning sickness, discomfort, and the birthing pains that bring this little sibling into this world. During the time of new levels it can become very uncomfortable.

But after the child comes there is great joy! Because of God's greatest miracle, she now forgets about the pain, discomfort, and sickness, and focuses on the result of her labor. So it is with spiritual birthing. God challenges us to enter into new levels. His vision is conceived in our spiritual womb. As vision grows and gets close to birth, we become more uncomfortable. We can easily lose vision in the process due to the length of time it is taking to complete. But when the baby *(vision)* comes, it is worth all that you had to go through.

Joshua was faced with the new challenge of taking the people over into Canaan Land. They had never been that way before. It was new to him. It was uncomfortable to him. It was

Moses who was always talking to God. It was Moses who was always getting the direction. But now, things had changed. Moses was dead! (Joshua 1:1) God had taken Moses to his final destination and Joshua became God's mouthpiece. Joshua's spiritual birthing had now become a suddenly. He was the point man that was now responsible for new direction from God.

Joshua 3:4

...for ye have not passed this way heretofore.

As believers being truly called of God, we too must be willing to allow God to move us out of our comfort zone in order that His will might be accomplished. Joshua's comfort zone was being with Moses and allowing God to deal with Moses and not himself.

STAYING IN THE COMFORT ZONE

There have been many Christians and ministers alike that have never achieved their destiny due to being afraid to leave their comfort zone. Sometimes a person becomes so comfortable having the ability to overcome their daily challenges they stay the same day in and day out. They get up every morning, eat the same breakfast, usually at the same time; get in their usual car; drive the usual route; wave at the same person on the corner; and usually arrive at the same desired time if the traffic has not changed. It is called a rut!

> We have become creatures of habit.

It was said by someone that the only difference between a rut and a casket is the rut has no ends to contain you. We have become creatures of habit. We sit in the same pew or chair at church and get mad when a visitor sits in *"our"* place. We get upset because someone has parked in our parking space. After all, I have parked in the same spot every Sunday for three years now! I own that spot! It's mine! I helped with the finances that paved that parking lot. I have tithed every week now. I can't believe that someone would be so disrespectful and park in my spot!

God will always use someone or something to get you out of your comfort zone. Just because someone parked in your favorite parking space or sit in your favorite chair, be flexible. All parking spaces are usually the same size and the chairs are usually the same structure in color and padded hopefully with the same amount of foam. Sometimes being out of your comfort zone strengthens your character and forces you to embrace your present surroundings.

When Elijah's provision had dried up, he was willing to hear the voice of the Lord again.

Just as Elijah had a comfort zone (being the brook Cherith), (I Kings 17: 1-6) we too have them. For Elijah it was provision and comfort. He didn't have to go anywhere; the raven brought him food and he had all the water that anyone ever needed. But suddenly there was no provision. There was no water. What had happened to God? Had God forgotten that He had told Elijah to go there? Surely God would not send somebody to a place without provision! It couldn't be God's fault that the raven did not come! It was that dumb bird that forgot to bring Elijah his provision. After all, who has ever heard of a bird bringing mankind any food? And rivers dry up all the time. Elijah's blessing must have just run out. Nobody can stay in the stream of blessing forever, right? No! God had allowed it all in order to get to Elijah to the next level.

Sometimes we picture God as someone who would never cut off our supply. We confess; that He is Jehovah Jireh. He is our provider. Providers don't cut off supplies, they provide.

As previously discussed in an earlier chapter, during a purging process the Lord usually provides. If the enemy is doing the testing, there is never any provision. But be careful not to move too quickly and allow your discernment to jump ahead and start binding and loosening. God could just be moving you to a new location in order to fulfill the vision and purpose of the Lord. Just because your provision dries up in one place, doesn't mean that the Lord will not provide for you in the next place.

But if we could stop for a moment and allow ourselves to see what the Lord was doing for Elijah, we would notice that Elijah was on the run. He had no place to go. He had no place to hide. And suddenly the Lord spoke to him and told him to go and hide by the brook Cherith. It was a place of provision. But when the river dried up Elijah began to become uncomfortable.

Would God treat us any different today? First of all we must be willing to hear His voice. If we can't hear His voice, then we must place ourselves in a place where God is speaking. When Elijah's provision had dried up, he was willing to hear the voice of the Lord again. Why, because it was the Lord that told him to go there in the first place. If God told him to go there, then God was big enough to move him on to the next place where there was provision.

We are placed in similar circumstances at times not knowing that God has placed us in a place of provision. We are there for a while and become comfortable and suddenly everything around us becomes foreign. "My boss doesn't like me any more. Everybody is getting a raise except me. The company took away my expense account. I can't look for a new job; I like this one. I have been here for over five years. Surely God would not have me move again. I am going to have a meeting with the boss; he is missing it. I can hear God and he can't." All these thoughts may rush through your mind while you are under pressure. Like Elijah of old, we too must enjoy the provision even though we don't fully understand the circumstances.

Have you ever been there or at least knew someone that was in that position? God began a new process in and around Elijah so that he would move on toward his destiny and fulfill vision. His comfort zone had dried up and Elijah was given his transfer papers. Now he was with no water, no food, no bread, but God spoke. Go to Zarephath. Elijah goes in obedience, not knowing where his next meal will come from, but willing to do as the Lord had told him.

Elijah is now heading toward his next level and approaches the gate at Zarephath. He meets a lady gathering sticks so that she could cook her last meal and die. Elijah cries out *"give me some water"!* As the little lady was going she hears another cry from Elijah. *"Bring me some bread that I might eat"!* The lady stops and turns around and Elijah hears his first bad news of the day. Elijah did not need to hear any bad news. He was thirsty. He was hungry. He was being obedient and God sends him to a lady who had nothing. Elijah was in a purging process that would not only change his life, but also change the life of those around him.

The lady spoke out, "I don't have any bread. I have only a handful of flour and just barely enough oil to cook with and after that, my son and I are going to die."

Now we see another process in motion. The Lord has moved Elijah from one process to another. He moved him from great provision, to providing for someone else. It was his obedience to God, and the ladies obedience to Elijah, that brought the provision through God for both of them.

If we will stay obedient in the midst of our process, God will always see that we not only help ourselves but others around us as well.

We are witnessing a time where we must cross over into our promised land even though the Church has not gone this way before. The Church is moving into a new spiritual era and must boldly take its rightful position. Even though we as a body of Christ know that there will be challenges, we cannot be disobedient and remain where we are comfortable. Jesus came that we could have the freedom, not to continue in the doctrines of man, but to embrace the holiness of God and destroy the forces of evil.

1 John 3:8

"He that committeth sin is of the devil; for the devil sinneth from the beginning. For this purpose the Son of God was manifested, that he might destroy the works of the devil."

It is so interesting to watch saints and converse with them as they mature in the body of Christ. They are filled with the zealousness of Apostle Peter, but when they begin to go through a *perfecting*, they believe everything is always the devil.

> *The Church is moving into a new spiritual era and must boldly take its rightful position.*

Without defending the enemy, let me evaluate a spiritual issue. I believe the enemy should be put under our feet every time we get a chance. Also I believe we should bind and loose and question everything that looks or feels like the enemy...but we must be careful not to react too quickly and focus our prayers toward the camp of the wicked. It is just possible that our attack is not of the enemy but it is God bringing us through a *perfecting*. How quickly we react to every little trial or tribulation and spend countless hours defending our spiritual awareness called discernment. Our discernment is the gift that evaluates good or evil but should not get in the way of God bringing us into greater provision.

Hebrews 5:14

"But strong meat belongeth to them that are of full age, even those who by reason of use have their senses exercised to discern both good and evil."

Elijah could have prayed, fasted, threw dirt over his head, prayed in tongues, cried, laughed, and even dug a hole for water, but it wouldn't have done him any good. His provision was in obedience and not in works.

As a prophetic people, we should use great wisdom and discernment to keep ourselves on the cutting edge. The Lord can put anyone in transition for provision at any time. When our surrounding becomes uncomfortable we must ask ourselves these questions. *"Is this a process to launch me forward or is this the enemy trying to steal my blessing?"*

For some career minded saints, God has to literally shake the ship in order to get them unchained from their present job.

I once knew a gentleman who was employed at his present job for over fourteen years. He was stable. His salary was great. His position was secure. He was on his way to retirement. Suddenly one day he became so uncomfortable, he began to hate his job, position, and salary. Upon being obedient to the Lord, he gave his resignation. Everyone thought he had lost it. There wasn't anything wrong with his workplace; the Lord had to dislodge him from one place in order for the blessing to come.

If God had not closed the door to his present employment, he would have probably retired there. Little did he know the future that God had planned for him.

After a few weeks of being unemployed and uncomfortable, he was saddened at the thought of quitting his career job. He was feeling hopeless and unsuccessful. Then suddenly that telephone call that he had prayed for came. A businessman called and offered him a job that doubled his salary and it was exactly what he had been praying for during his weeks of unemployment. There was even an increase in the benefits. Through all of his burden and uneasiness, God had come through.

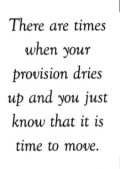

There are times when your provision dries up and you just know that it is time to move.

There are times when the Lord allows you to just be obedient even though everything seems to be going well. Then there are times when your provision dries up and you just know that it is time to move. Either way, it all seems to point to obedience.

All progression in the kingdom of our Lord does not have to come with a pearl of great price. Some theologians may differ with that statement but an opinion is still an opinion. If a person has gone through much tribulation and has gotten the victory, then yes, that process came with a great price. But if the Lord shows His great favor upon you, and you receive a breakthrough physically, financially, or spiritually, it could come just as a blessing from God. Sometimes we don't deserve it but because He chose us and we have believed, then He became our Father and Father's give good gifts.

James 1:17

"Every good gift and every perfect gift is from above, and cometh down from the Father of lights, with whom is no variableness, neither shadow of turning."

Sometimes when the Lord is bringing us into fresh "vision" it is easy for our minds to quickly focus upon the negative. Even though spiritually we may have never been in this position before, we must take control of our spiritual thoughts. After all, we have been planted upon this earth to rule and to reign with the power of the blood of the Lamb. Every time we receive a new revelation from the Lord, we go through a *process* of maturing in fresh vision.

NOT BY OUR OWN MIGHT

I learned a term years ago that keeps me abreast of the surrounding spiritual atmosphere. At every new level and promotion from God, there will be new devils. New levels - new devils! With every revelation from God comes a greater amount of authority. We can't fast enough, pray enough, or be holy enough to be used of God. We get promoted simply out of his goodness and mercy. Without goodness and mercy of God, we all would still be treading out the mud pits in Egypt. With God all things are possible. It is "I" who is unable to do anything on my own.

Throughout the Old Testament and into the New, we see humanity *(in his own ability)* unable to overcome. Adam could not handle his authority spiritually or physically. David being chosen genetically as the lineage of Christ could not stop his flesh from falling short of God's glory. Chosen generation after chosen fail short because they tried to overcome in their own power. And on and on it goes.

Even in the New Testament we see the Apostles helpless when trying to cast out demons. (Matthew 17:19) They come back complaining to Jesus of how their authority did not work. So, for someone to say "I" overcome would only be setting himself up for failure.

Progression can only take place when we realize that it is not by our power or might but by His Spirit. Jesus came and gave the Church dominion as long as we would continue to submit ourselves to the holiness of God. Our progression through the righteousness of God can only continue if we follow His ways. It is not who we are, but *"whose"* we are that makes the difference. As our spiritual progress follows Biblical order, we can expect the spiritual blessings of the latter rain.

When we are in the middle of our maturing process, it seems that no one cares if we survive. It is in that very moment that God's anointing is working. God looks upon us and while we are pounding out our territory, batting the air, fighting our good fight of faith, going nowhere on our own; suddenly His favor shines upon us. It's a breath of fresh air. Just when we thought we were going to sink, God calmed the waves. The boat stopped rocking. The storm stood still. Once again we know if it had not been for our Lord we would have drowned.

FROM GLORY TO GLORY

The Word says that we move from glory to glory.

2 Corinthians 3:18

*"But we all, with open face beholding as in a glass the glory of the Lord, are changed into the same image **from glory to glory**, even as by the Spirit of the Lord."*

We quote that verse like the glories run together, but actually it reads; from glory tooooooo glory. We forget that there is a process between the glories that could take years. This too is another one of God's maturing tools.

He is never late. Sometimes we think that God is nowhere to be found, but *suddenly* we are pulled out of the water and placed upon dry land. Suddenly there is a fourth man in the fire. Suddenly the Red Sea opens. Suddenly the enemy is killing off their own soldiers. Suddenly God speaks and new direction is at hand. Even though we feel as if we did not gain any ground, God smiles upon us knowing that once again we held to the very thing that keeps us going, our faith in Him. When vision is lost we often find ourselves traveling backward. We must hold on, even in the darkest of times, to the very vision that keeps our progression going forward.

> New levels -
> new devils!

KEEP THE FAITH

When you feel that you are losing vision, let me say that your *process* is not that much different than anyone else. Your battle is very much like everyone else's. Oh yes, some hide it better than others, but believe me, when God is doing the elevating; the process has a completion date. Everything that the Lord begins, He has already completed the ending. Learn to fight through your challenge. Even when you don't know if it is the enemy testing or if it is God doing the purging. One thing for certain you can rest assure that you will win in the end. You just have to make it to the other side without sinking.

If you seem to be the only one that has to tread water, it is probably an area in your life that the Lord is trying to perfect. Some will not admit that they have any problems, declaring that they have already been through that challenge. But that doesn't mean that they have completed the race. Many seem to offer great advice even though they have never been challenged with your situation. There are some challenges that have to be battled alone. Then there are those that need all the prayer that the intercession team can give you. For the most part, God knows you a lot better than anyone else. That is why the Lord custom designs the Christians process so that we will come to Him for the answer. You would not take your Chevrolet to a Ford dealer for repair. You would not take your dog to your family medical doctor. Instead, you would take the dog to the vet, and of course your car would be taken to the proper dealership. So, when we have challenges, we should take our problems to the one who knows the answer before we ask.

Matthew 6:8

> *"Be not ye therefore like unto them: for your Father knoweth what things ye have need of, before ye ask him."*

Have you ever wondered why we exhaust ourselves trying to solve most of our problems when it would be much wiser to cast our cares upon the Lord? I believe that the Church has overlooked the wisdom of Christ for almost 2000 years. He is the great counselor. Oh yes, we call upon Him but sometimes it is too late. The harm has been done, and now we want Jesus to pull us out of the hole. Yet we wonder why there has been little productivity in the kingdom of God. He is all-powerful and

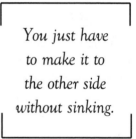

You just have to make it to the other side without sinking.

all knowing. One of the major reasons Jesus came to this earth was to dethrone satan, the god of this world. And by the way, He was very successful.

We too can be very successful when it comes to fulfilling our vision and destiny. As we proceed toward our new levels we will always be challenged. The enemy does not want us to finish the race. We should battle *through* the maturing levels, study to show ourselves approved (II Tim. 2:15), and give God the glory in the end. Remembering that it is the Lord that has entrusted to us a vision that only we can fulfill!

▶ Prayer for Progress

Father, in Jesus name, I am putting you first in my life from this point forward. I am tired of the enemy wearing out the saints and I am tired of fighting this battle alone. I unite myself with the Word of God and my spiritual family of God and declare the goodness of God over my family and me. No longer will I sit on the sidelines and watch my natural family nor my spiritual family be torn apart by allowing the enemy to wear them out. I decree in Jesus name, that from this day forward, I will do what I can to sound the alarm on the forces of hell on any principality that tries to seclude a believer in Christ. We are an army that sticks together. The enemy tried to seclude me from my blessings, but it has now backfired on him and I have become wiser than before. I will work smarter and not harder. The enemy is a liar and the father of all lies. I have found out his methods of seclusion by causing loss of vision and hope, therefore, secluding themselves from the very thing they need. Thank you Jesus for loving me. Please forgive me for my selfishness and pride, and forever thinking I could make it alone. Lord I not only need your help, but I need the help of my friends and those that are in authority over me. Thank you Lord for never leaving me for forsaking me. I am healed in my heart and my mind. AMEN!

CHAPTER SIX

RECOVERING THE LOSS

As your vision returns, one of the sly attacks of the enemy will be to tell you that you have lost so much ground that you cannot go back to where you were before you lost your vision. The enemy will try and convince you that you no longer have friends in your church or bible study. He will try and put thoughts in your mind that they know all about your problem so just throw in the towel and move on to another place.

Regaining your vision means the enemy will only try to find another route to come against you. During the period of regaining your vision and recovering your lost ground, it is helpful to have someone to whom you can express your feelings.

DON'T SECLUDE YOURSELF

One of the enemy's methods is to separate you from the friends and support system that you have had all along. He never seems to lighten up! If he doesn't succeed one way, he will attack in another area of your life. He knows that if one can send a thousand to flight, two can send ten thousand to flight. You may have not made the commitment to yourself or your friends yet, but that is something that you must do immediately. Don't stay secluded. Remember, it is the banana that is separated from the bunch that gets eaten!

The commitment that you make to yourself and to those around you will help you in your recovery. The Word says that we confess our salvation in order to be saved. Use the same principle and confess to someone that you have had a breakthrough and that you are on your way up.

Recovering from loss of vision can be very challenging. We do things that we don't normally do, and we separate ourselves from the very friends that are good for us. But because the enemy makes it so inviting and we believe the lies and become hoodwinked, we make unwise decisions.

Regaining your vision means the enemy will only try to find another route to come against you.

When recovering from loss of vision, one must take a good look at past experiences in order to learn from them. If we do not learn from our past, we will find ourselves back in the same place weeks or months later. It will only be a matter of time before the enemy comes again to steal, kill, and destroy, and blind our vision.

We can only recover our losses if we are willing to return to the race. Just as Apostle Paul reached for the prize of his high calling, we too must reach out beyond our fears and trust the Lord, knowing that His arm is not too short to touch us. It is our vision that keeps us on track and our faith that keeps us moving forward. Apostle Paul said we must not just reach for the prize but also forget those things that are behind. We cannot allow the failures of the past to keep us from pursuing the destiny that has been placed before us.

GOOD FOOD AND GOOD PROMISES

One of the ways of recovering your loss of vision is to gain control of your flesh and get involved in a good local church. If you do not have a church home - find one! Good churches are not hard to find, but be sure that they believe in God the Father, the Son (Christ Jesus), and the Holy Spirit. There are many churches that have different names but each one should have a faith statement explaining their beliefs. If they do not believe that Christ came and died for your sins, then search for another church. The local church plays an important role in your destiny.

By now I know what you are thinking. *"I have tried the church-thing and everybody there seems to have it all together."* Let me share something with you.

The people in the churches are not there because they have it all together, they are there trying to get it all together. This is only another lying trick of the deceiver. If the enemy can continue to convince the world that everyone in the church is holy, righteous, and pure; then he continues to be successful in his endeavor of bringing separation to families all over the world. The truth being, that there are families and individuals in every church that need major counseling, deliverance and prayer. They are not attending church regularly so that they can fool corporate America, but are placing themselves in an environment of spiritual enrichment.

When a person eats three meals a day regularly, they tend to be in good health and their strength endures the hours of hard work. Likewise, your spirit man also needs a well-balanced spiritual diet so that strength and durability can take place during the week of temptations and trials. When a person does not attend a place of spiritual enrichment, their spiritual values *(spirit man)* decrease and the flesh will increase.

TURN ON THE PRAISE

When the enemy comes while we are regaining our vision, some may not have the stamina to resist the forces of darkness. Satan knows our weakness sometimes better than we do. Because a person tends to seclude him or herself for a season, let me give you the best tip that is possible when regaining vision. *Turn on the praise.* When a person is unable to pray his way back into the race because of lack of vision, praise becomes the solution. Praise is the one weapon that gives you a spiritual boost and places you back onto your feet. You do nothing but praise the King of Kings and the Lord of Lords and He does the battling for you.

In the book of Amos chapter 10, the statement was made that *"Judah shall plow"*. Judah means praise. Praise becomes the plow that breaks up the fallow ground and allows the incorruptible seed (the Word of God) to fall into fresh plowed soil and to later become a harvest. We must see that praise and worship is the plow that breaks open the hard places and allows the anointing to soften our hearts. The seed that falls onto the ground has a better chance of producing fruit when the soil is plowed and fresh.

When the people of Moab and the people of Ammon, along with the Ammonites, came against King Jehoshaphat, he had to rely on the word of the Lord. The Lord had spoken to Jehoshaphat and told him that a great multitude was coming against them from beyond the sea, from Syria. (II Chron. 20) But Jehoshaphat feared and immediately began to pray and proclaimed a fast throughout all of Judah. They responded in the greatness of the Lord and declared unto all in Jerusalem and Judah, *"do not be afraid"*. The Lord told them not to be afraid of the great multitude for the battle was not theirs, but God's.

2 Chronicles 20:15

"And he said, Hearken ye, all Judah, and ye inhabitants of Jerusalem, and thou king Jehoshaphat, Thus saith the LORD unto you, Be not afraid nor dismayed by reason of this great multitude; for the battle is not yours, but God's."

How interesting this story is because it is later said that the praise team won the battle and destroyed the whole multitude. The Lord simply told them to position themselves, go to the Wilderness of Jeruel, stand still and see the salvation of their Lord. All of the inhabitants of Jerusalem and Judah went and did as the Lord had spoken.

When they reached their destination they began to worship the Lord. As they and their families raised their hands and their voices with loud shouts and high praises, God was glorified in songs and hymns.

The next morning as they headed toward the battleground, Jehoshaphat appointed certain worshippers to sing unto the Lord. And as the worshippers lead the army into battle. The song that they sang was:

"Praise the Lord"

"For His Mercy Endures Forever"

I don't know if you have ever thought of it this way, but can you imagine what the enemy must have thought? You are heading into battle with your soldiers equipped with spears and bows, and the ones leading your foe are a bunch of Levites singing the high praises of God! What an incredible paradigm shift! From bows and arrows and spears -to praise. But even though this type of action may not make sense to our natural mind, we must remember that His ways are higher than our ways. As they *began* to sing and praise the Lord our God who is spiritual (John 4:24), ambushments were being set against the people of Ammon, Moab, and all who came against Judah. As the enemy stood up to make war against their opponent, they began killing off one another. And when Judah came to the place overlooking the battleground, they saw a multitude of dead people and not one escaped!

> *It is our vision that keeps us on track and our faith that keeps us moving forward.*

Now, can you imagine yourself just singing unto the Lord when the enemy comes and suddenly your opponent is crushed by the angels watching over you? WOW!! That's an awesome thought!

HAVING MORE THAN ENOUGH

The Word says that when the people of Judah came upon the scene, their spoils were more than they could carry. They found themselves in the midst of more valuables than they could haul away. They thought that they were going into battle, but because they believed God and were obedient, they found themselves in the middle of more than enough!

Most Christians have enough to pay their bills, buy food, put gas in their cars, and possibly even go out for lunch on Sunday. But God wants the believer to have *"more than enough"*! Not just so bills can be met, but to have enough to give away some of the blessings. If a person has more than enough money, then they can become a blessing to someone else. But for most families it is hard to bless someone else when there is not enough to go around especially when the kids need clothes or shoes.

> *Don't try to explain the spiritual away.*

In Jehoshaphat's victory, the spoils included precious jewelry, stones, valuables, gold chains, and much more. The Bible says in Second Chronicles chapter twenty and verse twenty-five, there was so much that it took them three days to carry away the valuables.

Isn't that just like our Lord? He causes confusion in the camp of our enemy and allows His saints to walk away with more than enough. When we are obedient to His Word, good things begin to happen.

Just think, we wake up one morning with all kinds of worries. We are off to work with different concerns and the more we think on these problems the more magnified they become. And suddenly the Spirit of the Lord interrupts our thinking process while driving down the freeway. We are praying silently and suddenly the Holy Spirit says, *"Give me those worries, I can handle them better than you can"*. Suddenly, there is peace in the air that you have never felt before. Our problems and worries seemed to have vanished. We find ourselves singing and prais-ing God. We pull into the parking lot of our destination and find that we don't have any problems! The very thing that we were worried about doesn't exist! The other problems that occu-pied our minds seemed to have vanished. Our hopeless situa-tion has turned into a happy occasion and we can't explain why but we know who intervened.

Listen; don't try to explain the spiritual away. Just begin to collect your spoil. God has gone before you and accomplished in minutes what could have taken you hours. Just keep singing high praises to the Lord.

When we begin to put the high praises of God before our troubles, Judah begins to plow. How awesome it is to realize that when we begin to praise our God, He goes to work. We cannot see with our natural eyes the spiritual work that is taking place. We believe by faith that our Lord is at work destroying the enemy. If He did it for Jehoshaphat, He will do it for us. Praise sets ambushments against our enemies.

The Bible says that on the fourth day, the people of Judah and Jerusalem went back to Jerusalem with Jehoshaphat with great joy, because the Lord had them rejoicing over their enemies.

So as they went home, they played stringed instruments, harps, horns, and trumpets. With high praises and loud shouts unto the Lord they celebrated their victory. And the countries all around heard how the Lord had fought for His people and they feared greatly.

Lift up a sacrifice of praise unto God and He will do the rest. I know some will say, "I don't feel like praying or praising!" It has nothing to do with your feelings. It has everything to do with obedience. Your flesh will always be weak in spiritual battles. Our battles are never convenient! They come at our weakest time, when we just want to be left alone with nobody telling us what we should do next. Have you ever been there? The enemy seems to watch us and at the moment everything seems to be going great, he releases the hordes of hell. Or at least it feels that way. Be comforted in the fact that you are not the only one that has ever lost vision and you will not be the last. Don't allow yourself to feel alone in this, know you are going to higher level.

RISE UP AND FIGHT

We must be determined to regain vision. When we find ourselves drifting away from the destiny that God has placed before us, we must rise up and fight. Our minds must be renewed, our flesh must come under submission to our spiritual authority, and our thoughts must line up with the Word of the Lord that says, "I am more than a conqueror".

During the process of our recovery, we are able to take away from our battles, more than what we had before, if we will let God do the fighting. Jehoshaphat may have gone to battle, but upon arrival, he did not have to fight. His biggest task was to carry his valuables back home. He sent Judah first and returned with joy and an abundance of wealth.

A person may lose vision, but when recovering from loss of vision; you do not have to start all over by going someplace else. You can enter into your place of worship and not allow shame or fear to come upon you. The enemy has lost! He is mad, we are glad, but the victory belongs to our Lord. AMEN.

▶ Prayer for Strategy

Father in Jesus name, I praise your wonderful name. Your Word says in your name (Jesus), every knee has to bow its knee. Depression is a name, oppression is a name, fear is a name, shame and guilt is a name, and I declare by the wonderful name of Jesus that they must go. I pray for strategy from this day forth, and I will not give up because I am more than a conqueror. Lord I need your help and strategy in order for me to never be in a place of losing my vision again. It feels lonely and very depressing. The enemy has tricked me into believing a lie, but I have overcome by the blood of the Lamb. Lord give me strength to continue in your perfect plan and vision and I will help those around me to the best of my ability. Your Word says that hope deferred makes the heart sick. When I lose vision, I lose hope. Therefore, I feel as if I am unworthy to fulfill my commission. Give me strategies and discernment to see the enemy from far away, so I can defuse his plan before it becomes effective. Lord, I love you and thank you for never giving up on me, even when I gave up on myself. Give me a new song today that I may sing praises to you Name. Praise the Lord, His mercy endures forever! . AMEN.

CHAPTER SEVEN

KEYS TO RECOVERY

Let us sum up the final chapter by highlighting some of the main keys to recovery. We know that if the enemy came once, he will no doubt try again, but most likely try a different route. He is sly as a serpent but we know that God reigns and is much wiser.

KEY # 1 -- UNDERSTANDING VISION

First of all, understanding why God would even give us a vision is very important. Without an understanding of your purpose and vision, it is difficult for anyone to be victorious. In the book of proverbs, it says:

Proverbs 4: 7

"Wisdom is the principal thing; therefore get wisdom; and with all thy getting get understanding"

It was once said that if you don't know where you are going, any road would get you there. That is why Habakkuk said in chapter two that we should write the vision and make it plain.

It is one thing to have an idea of where you want to go in life, but it is another to write your vision tangibly so that you become stable in all your ways.

KEY # 2 -- DON'T SECLUDE YOURSELF

Another way that satan secludes the sheep is by telling them that they are not important and it would be a waste of time to call someone to get proper counsel because they are feeling secluded? CALL ANYWAY! That could be the most important phone call that you have ever made. Your vision is coming under an attack. Even though you may not feel as if your vision is directly under fire, YOU are coming under fire.

Isolation from your friends, natural family, and/or spiritual family can be a dangerous thing. When you feel as if you would be better alone than around your friends that should be a red flag for you. The enemy knows that one can send a thousand to flight and two can send ten thousand to flight. He knows that there is strength in numbers.

Deuteronomy 32:30

"How should one chase a thousand, and two put ten thousand to flight...... "

Offenses can come from tiredness, sickness, feelings, not having the right clothes to wear, not feeling needed, not having enough money, not having transportation, or feeling guilty because you can't buy a gift for the occasion, and other ways. Remember, if you give the enemy an inch, he will become your ruler.

> *When you feel as if you would be better alone than around your friends that should be a red flag for you.*

It is one thing to stay home because you are tired and common sense dictates that you need the rest, but it is another to seclude yourself because someone might ask how you are doing.

KEY # 3 -- TRUST, SOLUTIONS, & STABILITY

Experiencing transformation will require you stepping into a realm of trust. If vision has been lost, you will not be able to trust yourself at this particular time. Therefore it becomes necessary to entrust someone else to speak into your life even though you really want to be left alone. If you could trust yourself and think clearly, you would not be in the situation that you are now in. So you must trust someone else.

Associate yourself with someone that can give you some solutions and stability. DO NOT contact someone who will have pity on you. The last thing you need is for someone to come into agreement with you! If they are not spiritually stronger than you are, they will not be able to give you the quality answers that you need. Again, don't allow yourself to fall into agreement with someone that will only feed more fuel to the fire. You don't need someone to be in agreement with your condition, you need someone who can give you direction and solutions.

KEY # 4 -- BATTLE SPIRITUALLY NOT PHYSICALLY

We must always keep in mind that the enemy is a fallen angel and not God. There is only one true God and His name is Jehovah God. He loved us so much that he sent His only begotten Son (Jesus Christ) so that we can live a life of abundance. When Jesus was crucified on the cross, He did not leave us comfortless. He sent the Holy Spirit to teach us, comfort us, and empower us in warfare against the principalities and powers of darkness. We do not wrestle against flesh and blood (Eph. 6:12) but against principalities, against powers, against the rulers of the darkness of this world, against spiritual wickedness in high places.

Although the flesh seems to continue to fight spiritual battles, God's initial plan was never for the flesh to enter a spiritual battleground. Yes our bodies are a spiritual temple of the Lord, but Apostle Paul said that the spiritual and the natural would never understand each other.

1 Corinthians 2:14

"But the natural man receiveth not the things of the Spirit of God: for they are foolishness unto him: neither can he know them, because they are spiritually discerned."

1 Corinthians 15:44

"It is sown a natural body; it is raised a spiritual body. There is a natural body, and there is a spiritual body."

Have you ever gone to a baseball game dressed in a football uniform? You would look totally out of character dressed so differently. It is much the same when the flesh enters a spiritual battleground.

God did not make our flesh to battle against powers of darkness, because spirits of darkness and rulers of spiritual places are **spiritual** beings. The Word says that God is a spiritual being.

John 4:24

"God is a Spirit: and they that worship him must worship him in <u>spirit</u> and in <u>truth</u>".

We see that when spiritual warfare is being conducted, there are two main ingredients that we must use to be successful.

One of the two ingredients is truth. If we don't believe that all things are possible through our Lord Jesus, then we are already defeated. If you believe that you are sick because God wanted you sick, then you have missed the true meaning of the Word that says *"by His stripes you were healed"*.

First Peter 2:24 is only a continuation of Isaiah 53:5. The reason that Peter had to write; *"we were healed"* is because Isaiah had already spoken a prophetic word that we are healed. When God speaks a prophetic revelation, we must not religiously dissect His thoughts, but receive His Word as fact and promise. Jesus did not die for a few diseases or a few backaches; He died for <u>every</u> pain and <u>every</u> sickness.

When doing spiritual warfare; we pray, shout, sing, talk, or even act out the Word. The Word is our foundation that goes forth and conquers spiritually what we are saying physically. Our flesh only carries the Holy Ghost power being the temple of God.

Most of the time these attacks are manifested in the natural but are spiritual attacks upon our physical bodies. When someone does not understand spiritual warfare, it is a common mistake to handle the attack as if it was a physical rather than spiritual.

The second ingredient when in warfare is to know that God is a Spirit. (John 4:24) It is important for us to remember that God was not only in the beginning but was and is the beginning.

> *The last thing you need is for someone to come into agreement with you!*

If you are praising God with the high praises of songs and hymns, you will attract the hosts (angels) of heaven because you are lifting up Christ. But if you are negative, using destructive language, anger, being rebellious and have an attitude because you are having a bad hair day, then you will attract ungodly spirits. I pray that you are able to separate the difference spiritually.

STUDY YOUR OPPONENT

If spiritual warfare is to take place successfully, we are to wage war against the rulers, powers, and principalities, by spiritually discerning what we are about to battle. If our armed forces declare war in the natural, usually it is done after they have strategically studied their opponent. So it is in the spiritual.

We should not be too quick to rattle off some spiritual prayer against the airwaves of destruction. We must take into account that there is life and death in what we say and wherever we send our words, they will either be fruitful or destructive.

As the apostle James said, "Our tongues are little members but boasteth great things". (James 3:5)

I will use Acts 16 as an example. In this chapter we see Apostle Paul was walking down a street in Philippi. Suddenly a spirit of divination began screaming at him bringing great attention to herself. Apostle Paul turned and faced the enemy and used the authority of Jesus Christ and rebuked the spirit of divination. Immediately the spirit came out. Then the spirit began exposing itself through the leaders of the city. People began tearing Paul and Silas' clothes and beating them. And as the story goes, they were thrown into prison. At midnight they entered into a harp and bowl service, which was so anointed the earth shook. (Acts 16: 23 - 26)

If we could see into the spiritual realm, I believe that we would see hosts of angels waging warfare for them. I believe that our warrior angels are slicing and dicing the demonic spirits as we speak forth the Word. As we pray, sing, or shout out our spiritual battle against the forces of hell, angels go to work destroying the forces of the wicked one. Greater is He that is in us than he that is in the world. (I John 4:4)

Spiritual warfare can be a very complicated subject if we allow it to be so. The simple truth is we have the victory already but we must possess our territory. Just as the Lord had given the Israelites the land of Cannon but they had to go in and possess the land that was already given to them. We too must possess what is our land through the blood of Jesus. The key ingredients of spiritual warfare are faith, the blood of Jesus, the anointing, truth, spiritual wisdom, good discernment, and knowing Christ has died for you. As a believer in Christ, you have already been declared the winner.

> *When God speaks a prophetic revelation, we must not religiously dissect His thoughts, but receive His Word as fact and promise.*

KEY # 5 -- STRENGTHS & WEAKNESSES

You are the only vision holder of your vision. If the enemy can convince you to give up then your vision will die. Usually he lurks for the weakest moment of our life and when the opportunity arises, he attacks.

One of the things that the Lord showed me years ago was to learn your weaknesses and your strengths. When a person knows that there are weak areas in their life, they should immediately begin working on their weaknesses.

Have you ever seen someone who wanted to try out for the basketball team but had no athletic skills. They are unable to dribble, shoot, or even have a fundamental idea of what it takes to become successful in basketball.

On the other hand, this person could have great talent in soccer and become one of the finest players in the world. Their strength was not in basketball but soccer. Knowing our weaknesses and our strengths become vital tools when pursuing vision.

Dr. Bill Hamon, is the overseer and founder of Christian International and has written many books of spiritual wisdom. Dr. Bill told me once that if we leave our strength unguarded it can become a double weakness. Meaning, that the very thing we feel the strongest in, can become our greatest weakness when left unguarded. When we think everything is under control and we are untouchable by any force, we open a door through pride and suddenly we find ourselves in confusion and loss of vision.

KEY # 6 -- CHOOSE LIFE

When loss of vision occurs, there is a spiritual death that takes place. Your hope becomes deferred. Your joy seems to be lost forever. But don't give up CHOOSE LIFE.

When vision is lost, usually our thoughts don't line up with the Word. God has spoken by His Word that we are overcomers by the blood of the Lamb. We forget that our Father God knows all about us. Sometimes negative things are spoken because we are so deceived and blinded by the enemy that we cannot think positively. It is by choice that we choose to overcome. We must CHOOSE LIFE!

Our choices in life are an important role in determining

whether we are successful or unsuccessful in achieving our vision. Too often we learn too late what success really is. We count our lives as failures because we do not measure up to someone else's standard. Sometimes we count our successes before the final results have been completed. Choosing life regardless of our daily outcome is what strengthens our tomorrows. Without the vision and hope of our tomorrows, our today's become frustrated efforts to achieve something that is unreachable.

if we leave our strength unguarded it can become a double weakness.

As I stated in the beginning of this book, your vision is the very heartbeat that keeps you from perishing. When hope is deferred it makes the heart sick. When your heart is not in what you need anymore, separation becomes the tool of the enemy to pull you from the very people you need.

Regaining your vision can be a lengthy process or it can be an immediate thing. The real challenge is regaining it again. Your vision is part of your life. You must choose life in order to precede regaining vision.

KEY # 7 -- YOU CAN DO IT

Rebuke the enemy, pray for breakthrough, and set your thoughts on the Lord. With Christ Jesus all things are possible. In a short period of time your vision is regained and you will be destiny bound again with a life full of purpose and vision. You can do it.

May the Lord bless you and keep you.

PRAYER

OF THANKS

Father, right now in the name of my Lord Jesus I give thanks for giving me strength to regain my vision. I repent for giving the enemy power over my mind. I thank you for being with me all the while I was dwelling in self-pity. I know that you would never leave me nor forsake me. I am thankful for you sending friends my way when I need them the most. Sometimes Lord when I don't feel loved and appreciated, I know that you are always there to hold me. I cannot express my feelings sometimes but I am certain that you already know my weaknesses. Lord, without you, I would fall short of everything. But because I have received you as my Savior and Lord, I can be victorious in all things. My vision is restored and I am on my destiny track once again. Thank you Lord for rescuing me. I am truly blessed. AMEN.

PRAYER

OF SALVATION

If you have not received Jesus Christ as your Savior and/or Lord of your life, the simple way to do it is just call on the name of Jesus. He is faithful to meet you wherever you are. Just simply speak these words:

Lord Jesus, I am sorry, I don't know what to say so I am declaring by faith these words so that I can be saved by grace. I have made a lot of mistakes but I believe in you that you will wash away all my sins forever.

I confess you as my Savior and my Lord from this moment forward and renounce all other gods. I don't know how to live for you but I am willing to learn. I will turn from my sinful life style and serve you. Thank you Jesus for loving me enough to die for me. I know that if I were the only living being on this earth, you would have still died for me. I am turning my old life over to you so that I can receive a new start. I thank you that old things are passed away, and that all things will become new for me.

I am saved by faith and the grace in my Lord Jesus. I am saved! I am a new creature in Christ. AMEN!!!

Now call someone and tell him or her that you have just made Jesus the Lord of your life.

SCRIPTURES

FOR ENCOURAGEMENT

Philippians 4:13
"I can do all things through Christ which strengtheneth me."

John 8:36
"If the Son therefore shall make you free, ye shall be free indeed."

Philippians 1:20
"According to my earnest expectation and my hope, that in nothing I shall be ashamed, but that with all boldness, as always, so now also Christ shall be magnified in my body, whether it be by life, or by death."

Habakkuk 2:2
"And the LORD answered me, and said, Write the vision, and make it plain upon tables, that he may run that readeth it."

Proverbs 29:18
"Where there is no vision, the people perish: but he that keepeth the law, happy is he."

II Corinthians 1:20
"For all the promises of God in him are yea, and in him Amen, unto the glory of God by us."

Romans 8:1
"There is therefore now no condemnation to them which are in Christ Jesus, who walk not after the flesh, but after the Spirit."

Galatians 6:9
"And let us not be weary in well doing: for in due season we shall reap, if we faint not."

Ephesians 1:8
"Wherein he hath abounded toward us in all wisdom and prudence;"

II Corinthians 9:8
"And God is able to make all grace abound toward you; that ye, always having all sufficiency in all things, may abound to every good work."

Colossians 1:13
"We give thanks to God and the Father of our Lord Jesus Christ, praying always for you."

Hebrews 4:11-12
"Let us labour therefore to enter into that rest, lest any man fall after the same example of unbelief. For the word of God is quick, and powerful, and sharper than any twoedged sword, piercing even to the dividing asunder of soul and spirit, and of the joints and marrow, and is a discerner of the thoughts and intents of the heart."

Romans 8:28
"And we know that all things work together for good to them that love God, to them who are the called according to his purpose."

Hebrews 11:6
"But without faith it is impossible to please him: for he that cometh to God must believe that he is, and that he is a rewarder of them that diligently seek him."

Psalm 134:1-3

"Behold, bless ye the LORD, all ye servants of the LORD, which by night stand in the house of the LORD. Lift up your hands in the sanctuary, and bless the LORD. The LORD that made heaven and earth bless thee out of Zion."

Psalm 150: 1-6

"Praise ye the LORD. Praise God in his sanctuary: praise him in the firmament of his power. Praise him for his mighty acts: praise him according to his excellent greatness. Praise him with the sound of the trumpet: praise him with the psaltery and harp. Praise him with the timbrel and dance: praise him with stringed instruments and organs. Praise him upon the loud cymbals: praise him upon the high sounding cymbals. Let every thing that hath breath praise the LORD. Praise ye the LORD."

Matthew 5:16

"Let your light so shine before men, that they may see your good works, and glorify your Father which is in heaven."